MW00604935

The Mayflower

A Captivating Guide to a Cultural Icon in the History of the United States of America and the Pilgrims' Journey from England to the Establishment of Plymouth Colony

Free Bonus from Captivating History (Available for a Limited time)

Hi History Lovers!

Now you have a chance to join our exclusive history list so you can get your first history ebook for free as well as discounts and a potential to get more history books for free! Simply visit the link below to join.

Captivatinghistory.com/ebook

Also, make sure to follow us on Facebook, Twitter and Youtube by searching for Captivating History.

Contents

All great and honorable actions are accompanied with great difficulties, and both must be enterprised and overcome with answerable courage.

- William Bradford, Governor of Plymouth Colony

Introduction

The story of the *Mayflower* is a tale of extraordinary circumstances that made ordinary people into the founding fathers of an entire nation. And although the Pilgrims were far from perfect, with their condescending attitudes to non-Separatists and for Native Americans, it is difficult not to admire the sheer tenacity that it took to bring them all the way across the Atlantic.

Many of the *Mayflower*'s passengers originated from a small community in Scrooby, Nottinghamshire, where a radical group of religious reformers broke off from the Anglican Church and tried to establish a new way of life. Driven from their homeland by a vengeful king, they found themselves in the Dutch Republic, but even that couldn't be home to them. They needed to go somewhere entirely new, a place where they could build new lives and live as they pleased.

That place turned out to be North America. And so, the Pilgrims began their impossible quest to journey across the Atlantic, a voyage that would be as expensive as it was dangerous. There, they would start a new life on unexplored shores.

The story of the *Mayflower* is one of hope in the face of relentless difficulties. It's a story of survival, of fighting back against insurmountable odds. It's a story of sorrow, of thieving from an innocent nation, of invasion into a once-free world.

But most of all, the *Mayflower*'s story is a story about home: being driven from it, defending it, and seeking it. And you can read it right here.

Chapter 1 – The Pilgrims

The little ship climbed the wave gallantly, even though the towering wall of water loomed ahead of her like an impassable mountain peak. The sails were rolled up and tethered to their masts; to hoist those great rolls of canvas would be suicide in a wind like this. The wind drove directly into the eyes of the sailors as they frantically scooped buckets of water from the deck, hurling each one back into the ocean, only for another wave or blast of wind to send a shower of spray hurtling onto the deck.

It wasn't the spray that worried Master Christopher Jones as he wrestled with the wet and slippery whip-staff, which was a stick that helped to control the rudder. It was the wave they were climbing. The tiny ship's bow seemed to be pointing directly toward the stars or at least where the stars should be; instead, there was nothing but roiling clouds and darkness and the crest of the wave, white and terrifying, somewhere high above.

Master Jones clung to the helm. He wanted to cry some kind of warning to the sailors, but there was no time. They had reached the top of the wave, and with a sickening shudder, the ship's every timber creaking as though she would simply fly apart, the ship began to tip. Suddenly, they were plunging down, down, down into the black and inky heart of the ocean, into a trough that seemed so far below them that the ship was flying through the air instead of sailing on the water.

She couldn't make it. Surely not even this brave little ship could survive, Master Jones was convinced, as he clung to the whip-staff for balance as they plunged down toward the deep. She would strike that water and shatter into matchsticks, killing every soul on board. Those who didn't die on impact or drown in minutes would freeze in hours, slowly and in agony.

The ship hit the water again with a thump that knocked Master Jones from his feet. Sailors slid all over the deck, crying out in panic. Water slapped over the deck, washing icily around Master Jones's limbs as his feet scrabbled for purchase, but he had kept his hold on the whip-staff. He struggled back to his feet and squinted into the driving rain. Somehow, his sailors were still there. Somehow, the tiny ship had made it.

But even as a rush of relief filled Master Jones's veins, he looked up, and there was another wave, bearing down upon them, the little ship being driven onward toward it. Master Jones gripped the helm and gritted his teeth.

He wasn't sure how much more of this the *Mayflower* could take.

* * * *

The *Mayflower*'s journey brought her into an icy winter storm somewhere in the Atlantic in 1620, but its journey truly began more than a hundred years before, with a Roman Catholic monk who was tired of the church.

Martin Luther had long since dedicated his life to the service of the church and his God. Yet, even though he now wore the monk's habit and had taken the monk's vows, what he truly found in the belly of the Roman Catholic Church displeased him and smacked little of his idea of God. He saw the pope as corrupt, growing fat on the people's sins instead of helping to absolve them. In 1517, few people read the Bible for themselves, but as a monk, Luther was one of those few. He had copied passages of the scripture and dreamed of translating the Bible into German decades before it was ever translated into English. He wanted to make it more accessible.

Many of his fellow monks and priests, however, had other priorities, which were far less spiritual.

Luther's study of the Bible had led him to believe that sins had to be confessed, forgiven, and repented of. However, many priests of his time had other ideas. They believed that sins could be paid for in cold, hard cash instead. And since they were representatives of Christ on Earth, these priests believed that that money could go to them. As a result, they sold indulgences: certificates that stated that churchgoers' sins had been paid for instead of repented. While the ruler of Germany at the time, Prince Frederick III the Wise, had prohibited the sale of indulgences in parts of Germany, Luther was still confronted with members of his flock who would come to him with indulgences instead of repentance.

By October 31st, 1517, Luther could bear it no longer. He sat down to pen his *Ninety-Five Theses*—a series of demands upon the Roman Catholic Church to change some of its practices. In short, he demanded the reformation of the church, and so, the Protestant Reformation was born.

Outrage exploded across the European continent. The Roman Catholic Church was more than a religious organization at that time. In fact, its pope was one of the most powerful figures in the whole of Europe, wielding power on the same scale as emperors and kings. The church had a powerful alliance with and had crowned many Holy Roman emperors, who ruled over vast tracts of land, from Italy to the borders of Denmark. To allow a mere monk to change the church was for a ruler to kowtow to a peasant. Neither the pope nor many of the higher-ranking clergymen were going to bow to this lowly heretic, and in 1521, Luther was formally excommunicated from the Catholic Church. The same year, he was brought before the Holy Roman emperor himself, Charles V of Germany, who demanded he recant.

Luther would do no such thing. As a result, Charles V issued the Edict of Worms. Luther was formally labeled a heretic who could be murdered on sight by anyone who pleased.

Conflict broke out across Europe. Luther's supporters began to call for change; many of them were powerful men in high positions. A rift was torn in the very fabric of 16th-century European politics. This became known as the Protestant Reformation, and it sent ripples through time that we still feel acutely today.

One of those ripples was the Separatist movement in England—a movement that would lead to one of North America's very first European colonies.

* * * *

In the 1530s, the pope's power was crumbling all around him. Luther had issued his *Ninety-five Theses* more than a decade before, and he was still alive, well, and translating the Bible exactly as he had hoped. This gave rise to a shocking idea that was almost unheard of in Europe at the time: the pope could be challenged. And it wasn't long before kings began to stand against him too.

It was Henry VIII, King of England, who brought the Reformation to his green and pleasant land, but not in the way that many of its citizens had hoped.

Henry VIII, strangely enough, had once been a favorite of the Roman Catholic pope. Like most of his successors, he enthusiastically waged war with France over the province of Aquitaine, which had once belonged to England and had been won by France during the Hundred Years' War in the 15th century. The pope had given Henry his blessing for the war; in fact, if he could defeat the French, the pope had promised to crown him as the "Most Christian King of France."

All that changed with Henry's first of six marriages, which was to Castilian Princess Catherine of Aragon. Originally, Henry had not wanted to marry her, but his father's dying wish compelled him to do so, and they married just a few months after he ascended the throne in 1509. Henry was only seventeen at the time.

Like all kings of that era, it was absolutely important to Henry that he should produce a male heir—a prince who could bring not only continual power to the royal family but also the promise of stability to the entire kingdom. Having a well-trained crown prince waiting in the wings made a nation far stronger and more stable.

For the first ten years of their marriage, it seemed promising that Catherine might eventually produce a male heir. Her first child, a little girl, never took her first breath; she was stillborn. She produced a son in 1511, but the child only lived a little less than two months. This was followed by two more stillborn babies until finally, in 1516, she gave birth to a surviving child. But the baby, Mary, was of no use to Henry. She was a girl and could never carry the crown.

By the early 1530s, Henry had become desperate. Despite two decades of marriage, Catherine had failed to give him a son to bear his crown after his demise. With friction boiling across Europe, which was not helped by the Reformation that was steadily gaining ground all over the continent, Henry knew that to be a king without an heir was to place a target upon an entire nation. He needed a son, and if Catherine couldn't give him one, he needed to find another wife.

The trouble was that in 16th-century England, divorce was no simple task. In fact, divorce, as we know it today, did not exist at all. The only way for a married couple to be separated was annulment, which essentially meant that the marriage had never been valid in the first place. Henry needed to get his union with Catherine annulled, and the only person who could do that was the Roman Catholic pope, Clement VII.

Clement, however, refused. Not only was there no real reason for him to annul the marriage, but he was also firmly in the pocket of Holy Roman Emperor Charles V, who was Catherine's nephew. Even after Clement died in 1534 and was succeeded by Pope Paul III, Henry still had no luck with the Roman Catholic Church.

Many a man would have given up by that point. But Henry was a king of England, and he believed himself more powerful than some pitiful pope. If the Roman Catholic Church wouldn't help him, there was only one solution: he would have to create a church of his own, a church that would do exactly as it was told. And so, the Church of England was born, and instead of a pope, it had a monarch. And that monarch was Henry VIII.

While the split with Rome was undoubtedly a purely political move on Henry's part, it drew enormous attention from those with more spiritual motives. Reformers saw this as a chance to establish a new church that aligned more closely with their philosophies, one with a figure as formidable as the king of England behind it. For the English people who considered themselves "reformed," it was a chance to be able to openly worship the way they believed was right.

Unfortunately, for the Protestants living in England, it was not to be. Henry had little interest in changing much of the liturgy or philosophies of his church. He just wanted it to annul his marriage to Catherine so that he could marry the second of his six wives. As a result, the Church of England was similar in many ways to the Roman Catholic Church—a fact that many Protestants could not forgive. They believed that the Church of England needed to be dramatically reformed or purified, and thus, the English Protestants became known as the Puritans.

The brand-new church soon found itself under unrelenting pressure, and not only from the Puritans. Now that it was controlled by the king of England instead of a Roman pope, the church was considered his fiscal property, and Henry quickly set about plundering its coffers to fund his ongoing wars with the mainland. Monks and nuns found themselves hopeless, as churches were stripped of their finery, not only by Henry but also by Puritans who believed that worship should be a far simpler thing, one requiring no stained glass windows or golden statues.

But it was not the Puritans who would become the people who are the main focus of this book. The Puritans were moderate compared to the second group of people who opposed the Church of England. These were the Separatists, and one of the first among their number was a young man by the name of William Bradford—a young man who would become one of the very first men to be called "governor" on the soil of the modern United States of America.

* * * *

William Bradford was born to a wealthy yeoman family in either 1589 or 1590. His father, William Bradford Sr., owned vast farmlands in the beautiful countryside of Yorkshire, and little William was set to grow up with everything he could ever need. He even had some noble blood running through his veins, which came from his paternal grandfather's side.

In fact, William could have had a very cushy life as another rich English yeoman who presided over vast tracts of land farmed by serfs—peasants who were little more than slaves. But it was not to be.

Tragedy struck very early on in young William's life. He would never remember his father, as William Bradford Sr. died when his little son was only one year old, leaving his wife, Alice, alone with a tiny toddler. Nonetheless, Alice was still young and still the heiress of her husband's vast estate, and so, remarriage was not an impossibility. One-year-old William was barely aware of his father's demise. But three years later, after a suitable period of mourning, four-year-old William's world was turned upside down when his mother remarried.

The name of William's stepfather is lost to history, but it can be assumed that there was no love lost between him and his new little stepson. As soon as the stepfather moved onto the vast Bradford farm, he wanted nothing to do with William, whom he must have viewed as a rival of sorts when it came to the question of the inheritance. Little William was unceremoniously packed off to live with his grandfather. He was a little child with no concept of what was happening, knowing only that he had been torn from his mother's arms, from the only home he knew. It would not be the last time.

William lived with his grandfather for two years. It can be assumed that some form of education was provided to the boy while he was with his grandfather; perhaps his life even improved a little. If he was living with his paternal grandfather, William Bradforthe, he might have even been in the court of nobility. Nonetheless, he didn't stay with his grandfather for long. When he was only six years old, his grandfather, too, passed away.

Confused and grieving, the little boy was sent back home again since he had nowhere else to go. His stepfather reluctantly welcomed him back into his home, and for a time, William was finally in his mother's arms again. This, too, was short-lived. It seems almost impossible to believe that yet more tragedy could afflict such a young life, but when William was only seven, his mother passed away.

His stepfather had tolerated William's presence in the home only to humor Alice. Now that she was gone, he had no reason to keep William anywhere near him. The boy was sent away to live with his uncles in Nottinghamshire. While the journey south was not a long one, it was still a whole new world for William.

To make matters worse, little William was a sickly child. Perhaps as a result of the grief that had so cruelly assailed him, he suffered from a chronic illness that has gone unidentified by history. It confined him to his bed and rendered him far too weak to work on his uncles' farm.

Instead, William began to read. In 1560, thirty years before William was born, the Bible had been translated into Early Modern English in a version known now as the Geneva Bible. This was the first mass-produced English Bible, and it fueled the Protestant movement that was sweeping through England, as people found themselves accessing the scriptures themselves instead of through the medium of priests. Most Geneva Bibles were destroyed in 1611 after the King James Bible was published, but that was still years in the future. During William's early life, the Geneva Bible was one of the most readily available books in the country.

Even though William was only about eight years old, he was quick to reach for the Geneva Bible in his boredom when he was confined to his room by his illness. Even at his tender age, he quickly found himself absorbed in the contents of the book. Soon, he began to grow interested in other classical works, and he began to grow more and more fascinated by Christianity.

At the same time, change continued to sweep across England, even during the reign of Queen Elizabeth I, who has long been lauded as one of England's most astute rulers. Her rule brought peace to much of England, and while the Church of England was still integral to her government, Puritans soon found that some lenience was extended to them. They began to cautiously build small churches in the countryside, and soon, they had preachers of their own. The Protestant movement was gaining a real foothold in England, spreading like wildfire over the green hills of Yorkshire.

It was inevitable that a child as intelligent and curious as young William Bradford would eventually come into contact with reformed beliefs. William had been bounced from home to home and church to church, and he had never found himself feeling quite at home in the Church of England. What was more, the uncles who were caring for him were not particularly interested in religion of any form. They were interested in farming, and as soon as William was well enough, they put him to work on their farm just like any other boy his age.

It was around 1602 that one of William's friends came over and told him that someone was going to be preaching new and radical ideas in a nearby town. This was a Puritan preacher, one Reverend Richard Clyfton. Clyfton was a Puritan minister who was determined to bring his preaching across rural England. William's interest was immediately piqued. He agreed to go with his friend and hear Clyfton's preaching, and it changed the course of his life almost instantly.

Despite the fact that his uncles expressly forbade him from attending any more Puritan meetings, William was fascinated by them, and he continued to attend them anytime he could. Soon, he was becoming a firm part of the Puritan congregation in Nottinghamshire, and it was among them that he found the first real father figure in his life: William Brewster.

More than twenty-five years William's senior, Brewster first tasted the Reformation in the Netherlands during his travels with his employer at the time, an ambassador to the Dutch. His convictions grew increasingly Puritan when he returned to England, where he worked as a postmaster and, later, as a bailiff in Scrooby, Nottinghamshire.

By the time little William Bradford went to hear Richard Clyfton preaching in Scrooby, Brewster was a firmly established figure of the Puritans. He took pity on young William; the boy always came to the services alone, and it was clear that he had no real parental guidance in his life and had already suffered much and lost many of those closest to him. Brewster was kind to him, and he became a friend, mentor, and paternal figure to young William—one that would prove indispensable in the many trials to come.

The trials grew abruptly worse with King James I's ascent to the throne in 1603. Unlike the moderate Elizabeth, James was determined that the Church of England should control the religious lives of every soul in his kingdom. By this time, there were many small, independent Puritan churches throughout England. For James, this was a dangerous prospect. The Church of England was intricately linked with his kingdom's government, and to defy the Church of England was to defy the king too. His solution was the same as that of political and religious leaders across Europe. If the Puritans didn't worship the way he wanted them to, they would be punished. Accordingly, he directed his archbishops to crack down on the still-illegal Reformation activity that was rapidly spreading across England.

While many English Protestants continued to believe that the Church of England could yet be purified, another radical sect of Protestants–among whom Reverend Clyfton was chief–began to realize that the Church of England was never going to change. Fellow Puritans were suffering deeply at the hands of that church, and these people began to believe that it was beyond saving. This wave of religious persecution saw Puritans labeled as traitors. They could be punished by utterly crippling fines; the penalty for failing to pay these fines was imprisonment. To make matters worse, there were rumors spreading among the Puritans that their brethren imprisoned in London were not executed. Instead, they were left to starve to death.

By 1607, all Puritan activities were forced underground. Instead of preaching in a church, Reverend Clyfton was forced to hold secret meetings. As always, William Brewster rose to the occasion by offering the manor house where he worked at Scrooby as a venue for these meetings.

Sometime during this period, the Scrooby congregation was joined by a most unlikely new friend: a former curate for the Church of England. John Robinson, a young man in his thirties, had served the Anglican Church faithfully until he was asked to accept King James I's request to stamp out the Reformation within his country. He refused to do any harm toward his Puritan counterparts, and as a result, he was thrown out of the Church of England. Feeling absolutely lost without a church to call his own, Robinson eventually wound up finding the congregation at Scrooby. While there must have been some tension between Robinson and his new brethren at first, he very quickly became one of their most valued, respected, and loved members.

During the secret meetings at Scrooby, the congregation decided that the Church of England could never be purified. They became Separatists and were determined to split from the Church of England forever and form their own church.

Young William Bradford, then sixteen or seventeen, had little interest in what his new congregation wanted to call themselves. All he knew was that he had finally found a real family in this group of people, people far closer to him than his two uncles, who still disapproved of his religious activities. The more persecution the Separatists faced, the closer William drew to them and the more he attended to their teachings. No threat of chains or fines would dissuade him from his convictions.

It was in the same year as the Separatists were formed that disaster struck. The archbishop of York found out about the secret meetings at Scrooby Manor. William Brewster, young William Bradford's close friend, was arrested and fined. Others were not lucky enough to be able to pay their fines; many members of the Scrooby Separatists were imprisoned for some time. Seventeenth-century English prisons were no pleasant place, and when these people were eventually returned to their congregation, they told terrifying stories about life behind bars and more rumors of Puritan prisoners being starved to death.

While the Separatists had hung on for years despite persecution, it was starting to become obvious to them that religious freedom was no longer an option in England. If they wanted to worship freely, they would have to leave their country behind. Accordingly, they began to consider emigration. But with the archbishop of York breathing down their necks, this would be no mean feat.

Chapter 2 – Searching for a New Home

Ninety years after Martin Luther wrote his *Ninety-five Theses,* the Reformation was still dividing kingdoms and countries all over Europe. Perhaps none were divided quite so literally or dramatically as the area then known as the Netherlands. For centuries, the people of the Netherlands, which consisted of modern-day Luxembourg, Belgium, and Holland, had been passed from one ruler to the other, from Holy Roman emperors to the duke of Burgundy and finally to the king of Spain.

In 1581, however, a vast rift was torn in the fabric of the country. Spain was still profoundly Roman Catholic at the time, while many Dutch people were growing more and more Protestant. This and other issues caused tensions to boil over in 1566, and the northern Netherlands battled their southern neighbors for fifteen long and bloody years until finally succeeding in gaining independence. This independence would only become *de jure* in 1648, but by 1607, the secession of the north and south was solid. The southern Netherlands–modern-day Belgium and Luxembourg–were still under the Catholic control of Spain. But the northern Netherlands, then named the Dutch Republic and what would eventually become the modern-day country known as the Netherlands, was very much Protestant.

At the time, few European countries could claim full religious freedom for Protestants. That made the Dutch Republic a huge attraction for many Protestant families and congregations displaced by all kinds of religious persecution. The Scrooby Separatists were no different. This influx of people from all walks of life was a small part of what would eventually catapult the Dutch into a position as one of the most wealthy and influential nations in the colonial era.

* * * *

Even though Reverend Clyfton and John Robinson had decided on a destination for their emigration, their troubles were far from over. In fact, they were only just beginning.

As William Bradford would soon find out, escaping to the Dutch Republic was no mean feat. For one thing, passage to the Netherlands cost money—money that many of the members of the Scrooby congregation just didn't have. After all, these were ordinary, rural people, farmers, and tradesmen; most of them were low on the social totem pole. For another, the English authorities were not going to simply allow these criminals to simply slip out of the country. The Separatists would have to be smuggled across the sea to the Dutch Republic at considerable cost and danger.

Nonetheless, the danger of staying in England quickly began to outweigh the danger of planning an escape. For young William, this was a monumental decision, but it appears it was one that he made without a second thought. Leaving England behind would mean the loss of many things that must have been dear to him: the few family members he had left, the countryside he knew and loved. It would appear that no other members of the Bradford family had joined the congregation.

Yet, in the five years that William had been with the Separatists, they had become closer to him than his own blood relatives. He wasn't about to let them go to the Dutch Republic without him. He decided to emigrate right alongside them, a decision that set his life on a path that would later take him all the way across the Atlantic.

Now, though, he just needed to get across the British Channel. To do so, he and several others had no choice but to place their lives in the hands of a smuggler they didn't know. These upright Puritans had had little contact with the criminal underworld, but now they waded into it, having no choice but to make use of illegal methods to escape persecution. They met with a sea captain who agreed to slip them across the channel in his ship—for a pretty price, of course.

William was among the group of people who embarked on the journey across the channel with the captain. It was late in 1607, and he was no more than seventeen or eighteen years old; he must have been absolutely terrified as they were loaded into the hold of the ship. But they never left the port. Instead, the captain betrayed them, calling the Anglican authorities on them. Enforcers for the Church of England rushed into the ship, dragged William from his hiding place, and hustled him off to prison.

The terrified Separatists found themselves locked up behind bars like thieves or rapists. Even though their stay in prison was ultimately brief, it must have been a frightening experience for these ordinary husbands and wives, farmers, and craftsmen. Their only crime was what they believed and trying to escape the country that refused to let them believe it.

One would perhaps consider it forgivable if the Separatists had renounced their beliefs and turned to quieter lives in the English countryside after being released from prison. Instead, prison only made them all the more determined to escape.

Over the next two years, the Scrooby congregation slowly trickled out of England in small groups, smuggled to the Dutch Republic family by family. William Bradford would only leave Nottinghamshire in 1608. This next attempt at escape was successful. This time around, a different captain made good on his word and carried young William all the way to the capital of freedom—Amsterdam.

* * * *

While the Dutch Republic offered religious freedom to the Separatists, it proved to be anything but a paradise. Although this new land allowed immigrants to build whatever churches they pleased, it still held plenty of troubles for the English Separatists who fled there.

The first was glaringly simple. These were ordinary English folk, most of them poor, none of them wealthy, and they more than likely spent every penny of their savings to reach the Netherlands in the first place. They had lost everything: their homes, communities, and, in many cases, parts of their family. They now found themselves in an alien environment, many of them with children to feed and households for which to care. As much as they wanted to build a church of their own—now that they were allowed to do so—they were immediately confronted with the simple necessity of survival.

William Bradford was no exception. In fact, nineteen-year-old William had nothing at all in the Dutch Republic: no knowledge of Dutch, no work experience, no real skills, and no family. As always, Brewster was the one who stood up for young William and took him in. William moved in with the Brewster family in Amsterdam, and he stayed there with them for some time.

Other key members of the Scrooby congregation also made it across to the Dutch Republic, including Reverend Clyfton and John Robinson. In fact, Robinson was becoming more and more important in the spiritual lives of the Separatists. He would later become known as the "pastor of the Pilgrims," even though he himself would live out the rest of his days in the safety of the Netherlands.

Amsterdam, however, quickly proved almost impossible to navigate for the Separatists. The city was bustling with Dutch people who needed to work as well, and these English speakers were automatically at a disadvantage when it came to finding gainful employment. The work they eventually did find was, for many of them, hard. Most of them may have been skilled craftspeople back in England, but now they were forced to take whatever they could get, and much of the work was hard manual labor that paid a pittance and was both difficult and dangerous. As a result, the children had no choice but to be sent to work too; children as young as six or seven years of age could be put to work in the textile industry. These families had come to the Netherlands to worship, but it felt to them as though they did little other than work.

Many of the Separatists ultimately decided to move out of Amsterdam, with Brewster, Robinson, and William Bradford being among them. The town they chose for their new home was a picturesque small town named Leiden. They hoped that this environment would be more akin to the world they had known in the village of Scrooby and that there would be land to farm instead of factories to work in.

Even in Leiden, things didn't improve immediately. The part of Leiden to which the congregation had relocated was called Stink Alley for a reason. It was a narrow little street, lacking the gabled churches and tall buildings of the upper-class part of Leiden, and it lived up to its unprepossessing name. It was a long way from the prosperous manor and the rolling fields of farmland that Brewster and Bradford were used to. Nonetheless, it had one key quality that beautiful England didn't: Stink Alley allowed the Separatists to believe whatever they wanted. Brewster continued to keep Bradford fed and clothed, and the family struggled on together, attending regular services led by John Robinson.

Still, their troubles continued. Even though an uneasy truce had been achieved between the Dutch Republic and Spain, it was more of a ceasefire than any real peace. The Dutch continued to demand religious freedom for Protestants in the Spanish territories, while the Spanish demanded the same for Catholics in Dutch lands. Even though there was no real violence in the Dutch Republic while the Separatists were there, it was evident that tensions were still on the rise. The Dutch were steadily building up a bigger and bigger navy, and there was news of battles at sea. It was evident that a renewed war was inevitable.

One Englishman, John Carver, had managed to hold on to a significant fortune, but he nonetheless suffered during those early years in Leiden. John Carver would later become one of the most important men aboard the *Mayflower*, but there are almost no records of his early life. In fact, even his birth date and birthplace can only be estimated; he was likely born in England around 1584.

The first records we have that mention John Carver are sorrowful ones. He was living in Leiden with his first wife, a Huguenot named Mary, in 1609 when they welcomed their first child into the world. Tragically, the baby didn't live long. It was buried at the Walloon Church in Leiden in July 1609, and Mary herself followed not long after.

Now a childless widower, even though he was only around twenty-five years old, Carver was alone and grieving when he met a Separatist woman who would change his life, his faith, and his ultimate destiny. Her name was Catherine White, and she was Pastor John Robinson's sister-in-law. Catherine was as fervently Separatist as she was attractive, and it wasn't long before Carver fell head over heels in love with her and with her faith. He married her and joined the Separatist church at an unknown date in the 1610s. Even though he was a little late to the Separatist party, Carver would soon prove to be an avid believer, quickly becoming friends with Pastor Robinson and ultimately reaching the rank of deacon in the Separatist church of Leiden.

For William Bradford, things began to look up in 1611. He turned twenty-one and became eligible for the inheritance his father had left him. Somehow, despite the fact that he had left England illegally, he still managed to get his hands on the money. He was by no means rich, but it was enough for him to buy a modest house and set up a workshop on the ground floor, where he became a weaver of rough, cheap fabric used to make men's clothing. His life was perhaps a long way from his family's yeomanry, but it was an honest living. In 1613, he married a pretty English girl who lived nearby, named Dorothy May. The Separatist church had not written a marriage ceremony as of yet, so they were wed in a civil ceremony instead. Four years later, Dorothy gave birth to their first child: a little boy named John, perhaps in homage to John Robinson, who was still their pastor.

Many of the other Separatists were not so lucky. William Brewster, for one, had set up a successful Protestant press that produced anti-Church of England matter regularly throughout the late 1610s; these were proscribed in England as well, and Brewster often found himself under scrutiny from English authorities. He narrowly escaped persecution several times, most notably in 1619 when King James I's lackeys tracked him down and sought to kill him. The University of Leiden, however, was quick to protect him. Brewster had to be very careful for a while, but he was not imprisoned.

Yet, perhaps nothing was as hard for the Separatists as the change they saw in their children once they started to grow up in the Netherlands. By the mid-1610s, small children were becoming teenagers and seeking their own identity in the world. Like most young people, these children were more apt to ape their peers than their parents, and as a result, their parents felt that their English identities were slipping away. The young people picked up Dutch far more easily than the elders, and they were more accepted in the community, getting along with their Dutch neighbors more easily. It felt to the older Separatists as though they were losing their children and growing ever more alone in the world.

By the late 1610s, it was clear that a change would have to be made. The Separatists of Scrooby had no choice but to leave Leiden behind after a decade of living there. They needed to find a new home, a home where they would be allowed to live in peace. They needed to think completely out of the box. And they would have to find a whole new way of living.

What better place could there be to do this than the New World itself?

* * * *

By the time of the Scrooby Separatists, the concept of the New World was not quite so new anymore to the Europeans, but it was still largely unexplored. Even though it had been more than a century since Christopher Columbus stumbled upon the Caribbean islands in his quest for India in 1492, efforts to colonize North America had been largely unsuccessful.

Spain made short work of putting colonies in Central and South America, butchering and enslaving the native people as they went. But it was only during Elizabeth I's time that the English truly started to stake their claim in the New World, a land that had been inhabited for centuries by Native Americans. The English, like most Europeans, had no qualms about marching in and taking their ancestral homeland, and they started to found colonies there late in the 16th century. Elizabeth I had a keen interest in exploration, and her privateer, Sir Francis Drake, circumnavigated the globe in the 1570s. She also sent another courageous sailor off to North America in a bid to establish a colony for England: Martin Frobisher.

Frobisher sailed for North America, but he ended up stumbling upon Greenland instead, where he attempted to establish a small colony in a frigid bay. After this proved impossible, he headed for the coast of the modern-day United States, claiming it as "New Albion" for England in 1579. The naval powers of the Old World raced to snatch up their piece of land; England had to move fast if it wanted its part in invading North America.

Sir Walter Raleigh was the first Englishman to attempt establishing a permanent colony in North America. Sent by Elizabeth, he set sail for the coast of modern-day North Carolina in 1584. Together with a little band of 117 English people, he built a fort and named it Roanoke.

Understandably, the native people of the area—the Croatans—were less than pleased with this invasion. This group of English treated the Native Americans with arrogance and cruelty, and several skirmishes broke out between the colonists and the natives. Still, the colony held on for three years, long enough that its governor, James White, believed that it was time for more people to come to Roanoke and grow the colony.

He made the long and perilous voyage back to England in 1587 and ended up being stuck there, with absolutely no communication with the colonists, for three long years. White finally returned in 1590, and he expected to find a burgeoning colony of English people still clinging tenaciously to the wild world they'd discovered. Instead, he found an utterly empty village. Not a soul was left alive within it; there was only a single word carved into a post: "Croatan." This was the name of a nearby island as well as of the natives, and White held out hope that the colonists had moved to the island and abandoned their village. Although it is possible that is what happened, the truth is still unknown today. The colony simply disappeared.

During the rule of King James I, the first successful English colony was established. Unlike his predecessor, James was not interested in investing in land in the New World: instead, he wanted to make money off it as quickly as possible. As a result, he auctioned off strips of land on the coast of the modern-day United States, selling them to large companies in England. One was the Virginia Company of London, which was quick to stake its claim. In 1607, it sent a group of men and boys to modern-day Virginia.

They built a fort there and named it Jamestown, and almost instantly, they were assailed by countless difficulties. For one, the winter was freezing, and without the proper infrastructure, many colonists couldn't survive the cold. Another issue was disease, although it should be noted that the Native Americans suffered far more from the Old World diseases the sailors had brought with them. This was yet another reason for the Native Americans to resist the onslaught of Europeans into their land, and there were regular clashes between the Powhatan tribe and the Jamestown settlers.

To make matters worse, the Virginia Company of London was growing impatient with the lack of profits from Jamestown. There had been rumors that Virginia was rich with gold, yet miners had little luck finding any at all. Money and resources grew short as men died of disease and fighting, and the colony seemed doomed until 1612. That year, John Rolfe began to cultivate tobacco seeds from the West Indies in the rich Virginian soil, and the crop proved to be as popular as it was prolific. When the Jamestown settlers started exporting tobacco to England, the colony began to make money, and its future grew more certain.

John Rolfe would once again be an instrumental figure in Jamestown when he made peace between the English and the Powhatan two years later. In 1614, he married a Powhatan princess named Matoaka. She would go down in history by her childhood nickname, "Little Mischief," or Pocahontas.

The peace only lasted eight years, but it was all the time the colonists needed for Jamestown to grow into a successful and thriving settlement. By 1619, women were arriving by the shipload to join their husbands or marry new ones. The population began to grow, families were established, and the luckless Powhatan had to face the terrible truth: the Europeans had taken their land, and they were there to stay.

* * * *

The Separatists, like Bradford, Carver, and Brewster, knew by then that colonization was possible in the New World. Jamestown's success had proven that the English could find a foothold in the American wilderness. Still, the very thought of leaving the civilization they knew and traveling all that way into the unknown was still a fairly crazy one for many reasons.

The first was simply that this little group of English exiles was still largely penniless. Although John Carver and William Bradford both had made a fair fortune for themselves over the years, they were in the minority, and even they couldn't dream of singlehandedly funding a venture such as this one. There was a reason why James I had auctioned off the New World to the highest bidder: even the Crown didn't always have the budget for financing expeditions and new colonies. Large, wealthy corporations like the Virginia Company of London stood to lose thousands of pounds in failed colonies. Buying ships, supplying provisions for the voyage, collecting enough tools and resources to start civilization as the Europeans knew it from scratch on an entirely new continent—all of that cost far more money than the Separatists could even dream of.

Another problem was that the ordinary people of the Separatist community were not survivalists, adventurers, soldiers, or even sailors. They were just ordinary farmers and merchants; they had none of the experience required to survive in the hostile wilderness that was Virginia at the time. They would face the full wrath of Mother Nature in her rawest and purest form out there, not to mention the native peoples.

Simply put, it was unheard of for ordinary and often penniless people to simply decide they wanted to move to the New World. One only went there if one was sent by a country or a company. But the Separatists were certain of what they wanted. To them, their journey would be one of faith, and it is for this reason that they became known as the "Pilgrims" centuries after their historic voyage. They had no way of knowing that a nation would ultimately be founded on their shoulders.

Accordingly, the Pilgrims began to search for creative solutions to their problems. John Carver, now a very active member of the Separatist congregation, was one of the first to start negotiating and coming up with solutions for getting to the New World. By 1617, the same year he once again had to bury a newborn child, Carver was already starting negotiations with the English Crown for land in Virginia.

Asking an Anglican king, who had already driven them out of the country, to permit a Protestant colony on a whole new continent was already a significant obstacle. It was one that Carver ultimately overcame, but even that was less daunting than the sheer fact that the Pilgrims didn't have the money. They needed financing.

Seeking a solution, and with negotiations underway between Carver and the Crown, many of the Separatists began to move from Leiden back to England, once again living out their faith in secret in order to be in a better position to prepare for the voyage ahead.

William Bradford was among them. In 1619, he sold his house in Leiden and moved to London, taking his wife Dorothy and little John with him. Religious freedom was still a long way from coming to London, but it would seem that Bradford still managed to become a fairly successful merchant. He was one of the few Pilgrims capable of making a fair amount of money, but no matter how hard Bradford worked, he would never be able to make even a tenth of the amount of money necessary to take the Pilgrims to the New World.

Back in Leiden, John Robinson got to work encouraging and upbraiding his people for the next great step they were going to take. He considered America to be a "New Israel," a promised land flowing with milk and honey where they could build up a nation according to his beliefs. It was a fantastical idea, one that arguably never came to fruition. But it drove the Pilgrims to this historic undertaking.

Knowing that they needed the backing of some large company to finance the expedition, the Pilgrims approached numerous companies in the hopes of striking a deal. They were uninterested in profits; they just wanted to farm American soil and practice their religion in peace. While no single company was willing to take the gamble on this ragtag group of religious outcasts, a group of rich men led by Thomas

Weston decided that pooling their resources would spread the risk and still have the potential for a good return. They formed a group known as the Company of Merchant Adventurers of London and agreed to fund the trip to the New World provided that the Pilgrims furnish them with resources like furs, fish, and, especially, tobacco, which they would sell in Europe at a good profit.

The Merchant Adventurers invested the equivalent of half a million US dollars in today's money, and the Pilgrims were ready to begin preparations for their voyage.

Little was known about "Virginia" and its geography at the time. The Pilgrims knew that the Hudson River existed and that it ran out into the sea at a point hundreds of miles north of the settlement of Jamestown. Even though Jamestown was flourishing at the time of the Pilgrims' preparations around 1619 and 1620, the Pilgrims had no desire to mingle with the settlers there. The settlers of Jamestown were all loyalists to the English Crown, and the last thing that Bradford, Brewster, and the others wanted was to continue living under the thumb of the Church of England. While they would still technically be citizens of the British Empire when they moved to America, the Pilgrims knew that putting the Atlantic Ocean between them and King James' zealots would give them as much freedom as they had ever had in the Dutch Republic, if not more.

Eager to start establishing Britain's power in the New World, King James was suddenly far more amicable toward the Separatists when their plans were revealed. He finally allowed them to legally separate from the Church of England as long as they left peacefully.

Instead of settling in Jamestown, the Pilgrims elected to establish their colony at the mouth of the Hudson River, the location of modern-day New York City. That would put them at a safe distance from Jamestown and the Anglican Church's lackeys. They hoped to establish a peaceful little farming village, where they could tend tobacco crops to appease the Merchant Adventurers, build any kind of church they wanted, and raise their children to be both fully English and fully Protestant.

This dream had in large part been conceived by John Robinson, but like the biblical Moses, he would never set foot in the promised land himself. Robinson was an old man by the time the Pilgrims began their preparations, and he knew that the young and strong would have a better chance at surviving in the New World. Instead of joining the other Pilgrims, Robinson chose to stay behind in Leiden and minister to the English people who remained there. The plan was to ultimately relocate the entire Scrooby congregation to the New World; sadly, for Robinson, he would die before that plan ever came to fruition. Even though he himself never made the pilgrimage, he would go down in history as the "pastor of the Pilgrim Fathers."

Instead, a stalwart and faithful younger man would have to be selected from the Pilgrims' ranks to be their leader on the voyage and in their new home. The choice was easily made. Ever since he had lent out his manor house as the site for secret meetings back in Scrooby more than a decade ago, William Brewster had been one of the staunchest supporters of the Pilgrims' cause. From printing Protestant material in English to becoming a father figure to young William Bradford, Brewster had proven himself many times over to be a worthy leader.

Under his leadership, plans rapidly began to take shape during the first half of 1620. Now that they had procured finances, they needed two more things: ships and sailors to man them. None of the Pilgrims were particularly skilled in that regard. They would need a large ship to carry their congregants and supplies across the Atlantic, but they would also need a ship that could stay behind with them, facilitating fishing and exploration around the mouth of the Hudson. Still, even with the backing of the Merchant Adventurers, the Pilgrims' budget was still very limited. It was decided that they would lease the larger ship and purchase a tiny vessel, something barely adequate for crossing the Atlantic.

This smaller ship turned out to be the *Speedwell,* a sixty-ton English-built ship that had seen better days. Built in 1577, the *Speedwell* was already well over forty years old by the time the Pilgrims purchased her. She had been built for the English navy, where she had originally been named *Swiftsure,* and had survived plenty of action when war raged between the English and Spanish in the last few years of the 16th century. In fact, the *Swiftsure* had faced the might of the Spanish Armada and survived.

After the battles, the *Swiftsure* had been part of an expedition to the Azores, a chain of islands in the Atlantic near the coast of Portugal. She had been one of the first English ships to sail those perfectly blue waters, and she had done her country proud in exploration as she had done in war.

But that had been many years ago. She had been younger then, faster, and not in the decrepit state of disrepair in which the *Speedwell* was when the Pilgrims bought her. She had been decommissioned years ago, hence the change of name, and despite the optimistic moniker, the *Speedwell* was neither speedy nor did she go well at all. But she was all that the Pilgrims could afford. She was docked at Amsterdam, from whence she would take the Pilgrims who were still living in Leiden across to England and rendezvous with the larger ship.

The *Speedwell*'s name would largely be forgotten by history. But the larger ship's name would become recognizable all over the world, ringing down through centuries of history: the *Mayflower.*

Chapter 3 – The Passengers of the Speedwell and the Mayflower

Illustration I: A replica of the Mayflower.

Christopher Jones had no idea that his name would go down in history as the man who brought the Pilgrims to their promised land.

Jones had been born in 1570 to English parents in Harwich, Essex. His father, a trader, had been the partial owner of a merchant vessel named the *Marie Fortune*, and there may as well have been seawater in Jones's blood. The storm-tossed horizon had always called young Christopher's name, and so, when his father died and his mother remarried when he was only a teenager, there was only one place that he wanted to go: the open sea.

Jones was not yet eighteen when he first stepped aboard a sea-bound ship, and he quickly found the work addictive. With a whole new world to explore and trade bustling between England and the rest of the world, there was no shortage of ships on which a capable and driven young man could be given a job, and Jones made it his mission to making something of himself out at sea. He likely inherited his share of the *Marie Fortune* when he came of age; combining this with his hard work, Jones was determined to become a successful trader and seaman, just like his father.

It would take time, but Jones didn't quit. There was something about those tossing waves that he just couldn't get enough of. Still, it was only after his first wife, Sara, died in 1603 that Jones really started to reap the rewards of his efforts. He married his second wife, Josian, only a few months after Sara's death; not long after that, Jones finally made enough money to have his own ship built. She was a splendid thing, too, bigger than most mercantile vessels at 240 tons. He loved and admired her, and accordingly, he named her the *Josian*.

The *Josian* became the foundation of Jones's business sailing to and fro across the English Channel, exchanging Bordeaux wine for English wool. His fortunes grew, and so did his family: the human Josian proved to be just as fruitful as her naval counterpart, and she gave birth to four children over the next few years.

Meanwhile, as Jones was sailing back and forth across the channel and as his family was growing robustly in Harwich, a ship was being built in that very same port. History took absolutely no notice, and for good reason. This ship was one of thousands of plain old merchant vessels being built all over the world. There was absolutely no difference between this ship and all the others; it was of a mediocre size at around two hundred tons, and it had a perfectly ordinary design with three masts. Even its name was a common one; in fact, twenty-five other ships shared the same name. Its owners had dubbed it the *Mayflower*.

Christopher Jones, too, was becoming a well-off but thoroughly ordinary merchant captain. The *Josian* had made him a modest fortune, and Jones was earning a reputation as a pleasant man who had perhaps a little too much disregard for the law at times; he was fined for keeping a pack of hunting dogs, an activity that was legally restricted to only the nobility. Despite this, Jones was making good money, and his family was continuing to grow.

In 1609, Jones sold the *Josian*. She had served him well, but it was time for a new venture, and that venture proved to be a 25 percent share in a new merchant vessel: the *Mayflower*. She proved to be just as lucrative as the *Josian* had been, and Jones was contracted to take longer voyages out onto the open sea, including a long trip to Norway to bring back a cargo of herring and even a whaling expedition out on the ocean.

Over the next several years, Jones would captain the *Mayflower* through many trade voyages, carrying everything from hops to hats to Spanish salt and more. In 1611, he moved his family to Rotherhithe near London; here, Josian bore him four more children.

Life was good for Jones. Yet, there must have been a part of him that hankered for the open sea. And when Thomas Weston, an unscrupulous businessman and a chief member of the Merchant Adventurers, approached him with the opportunity to take the longest voyage that the *Mayflower* had ever attempted, Jones was eager to say yes.

* * * *

As much as the Pilgrims were strictly devout, most of the Merchant Adventurers were anything but. Thomas Weston was chief among them.

Weston had been born in 1584 and grew up to become an ironmonger. He proved to be good at his trade and quickly began to expand it, changing from having a simple ironmongery business to shipping cargoes across the English Channel and cutting every corner he could to maximize his profits. He often skipped out on paying customs, no matter what kind of fraud he had to commit in order to get this done, and he also had no scruples about transporting illegal goods to England and selling them there.

Perhaps Thomas Weston would have dealt in cocaine or heroin today. But 17th-century Europe had a very different form of contraband: Protestant books and pamphlets. The Reformation was sweeping across many parts of Europe, continuing to cause division everywhere it went, and word was spreading. Much of it spread by the hand of smugglers. The Puritans in England were eager to get their hands on more Reformation material, by any means, and Weston was all too happy to smuggle it to them—at a price.

It was through his work smuggling Protestant material to England that Weston ultimately ended up meeting the Pilgrims. One of his partners in crime married a Separatist, and so, Weston was one of the first English businessmen to get involved with the Pilgrims, helping to start the Merchant Adventurers.

He was also given the task of finding a ship to accompany the *Speedwell* to America. This one would have to be far bigger, one capable of carrying the people, resources, and livestock required to start a whole new life on a different continent, but it could be returned to England when the voyage was over. Accordingly, it was decided to charter the second ship instead of buying it, and so, Weston approached Jones to lease the *Mayflower* and her crew.

It's uncertain why Jones agreed to a voyage that was so different from anything he'd ever done before. The *Mayflower* was a merchant vessel and a small one at that; it was nothing like the strong ships that had made the long journey before. This venture was far riskier than simply moving wool and wine between England and France. Perhaps Jones had been out on the open sea before, back when he was just a teenager looking for his place in the world. And perhaps there was something about those untold fathoms of water, about those distant lands and vast skies, that could never be replaced by any amount of success or fortune.

The Pilgrims had finally procured two ships in which to travel to America, and their destination was set. Still, they needed one more thing: a military man to keep them safe. That man turned out to be Myles Standish.

* * * *

The Pilgrims were well aware that one of the greatest threats they would face in America would be the Native Americans. Even though a tenuous peace still existed between Jamestown and the Powhatans at the time, there was no guarantee that the indigenous peoples of the Hudson River area would be at all welcoming—a fact for which it is impossible to blame them. Even though the Europeans saw themselves as courageous explorers who were given a divine right to claim the New World for themselves, what they were to the Native Americans was something entirely different. They were just barbaric invaders, plundering their lands.

Fearful of the threat, the Pilgrims knew they would need military support. They also knew they couldn't possibly afford to hire mercenaries for their protection, but they would ensure they had at least one military man travel with them in order to keep them safe. The first man they approached was an obvious choice: John Smith.

Smith had been instrumental in the founding and protecting of Jamestown in its early days. In fact, it may not be too much to say that he almost singlehandedly ensured its survival. An experienced soldier and reckless adventurer, Smith had explored much of Virginia, and he would undoubtedly be well suited to the difficult task ahead.

What was more, when the Pilgrims approached him in England, Smith was anything but reluctant to return to the New World. However, the price he gave them was impossibly high. In addition, the Pilgrims found themselves disillusioned with the type of man this fabled explorer had turned out to be. He was everything that they'd heard—strong, fearless, experienced—but he wasn't a Separatist. In fact, the Pilgrims found him to be arrogant and overbearing, and they feared that appointing him as their military adviser would be to subject themselves to needless tyranny.

Instead, the Pilgrims decided to turn to someone else, a man that they knew personally: Captain Myles Standish.

Like John Smith, Standish wasn't a Scrooby congregant, nor is there any evidence that he ever became a Separatist at all. In fact, he had spent his earlier years putting his life on the line for queen and country. Born in 1584, probably in Lancashire, Standish had first seen action during the Dutch Revolt that had split the Dutch Republic from the southern part of the Netherlands. Queen Elizabeth I considered it more important to fight her lifelong enemies, the Spanish, than to oppress the Protestant Dutch Republic, and she allied herself with the Dutch in order to fight Spain. Standish was one of the many young English soldiers who would have their first taste of battle in the Netherlands.

Standish likely journeyed to the Netherlands around 1603, the same year that Queen Elizabeth died. Still, he would fight there for a year, likely under the command of Sir Horatio Vere. By the time the Treaty of London was signed in 1604, Standish had seen enough of the Netherlands to know that he wanted to settle there.

It's unclear where Standish spent the next fifteen years. It is possible that he traveled back and forth between the Dutch Republic and England a few times, but by the time the Pilgrims were making preparations to leave, he was living in Leiden right alongside them. Standish wasn't a part of the Pilgrims' church; in fact, he may have been an Anglican to his deathbed. Still, he was known, liked, and respected by the Pilgrims. What was more, he had risen to the rank of captain during the war with Spain, and he was still a capable military leader.

Perhaps most crucially to the Pilgrims, when they approached Standish with the offer of making him their military adviser, he accepted a far lower offer than John Smith would have even considered. And so it was settled: Standish and the Pilgrims would be sailing to America on the *Mayflower* with Master Jones.

* * * *

By the time the final preparations were being made, the passengers of the *Mayflower* had become an increasingly eclectic bunch. This voyage would not only be for the Pilgrims–Thomas Weston made sure of that.

The Merchant Adventurers had only one primary objective with the voyage of the *Mayflower*: to make money. They had already made a huge investment with the purchase of the *Speedwell* and the lease of *Mayflower*, and they were eager to start making an income as quickly as possible. There was one glaringly obvious way to do so: sell tickets to the New World. While the Pilgrims had, perhaps, hoped that only a handpicked group of Separatists would be involved in establishing their new colony, their hopes were quickly shattered by the mercenary agenda of Weston and the others. Soon, the *Mayflower* and the *Speedwell* were fully booked, and not just with Pilgrims but with anyone who could afford to buy their passage across the Atlantic. Or, in the case of the four More children, anyone whose parents wanted to get rid of them badly enough that they would pay for them to be taken to a different continent.

The More children would become some of the youngest passengers aboard the *Mayflower*, and their story was a tragic one from beginning to end.

It started with two fathers who cared little for what their children felt and more for the size of their estates. Richard More of Linley and his brother, Jasper More of Larden, each owned very large and lucrative estates in the English countryside. And while Richard had a healthy eldest son who would ultimately inherit his property—Samuel More—Jasper was not so lucky. His last son had been killed in a senseless and violent duel, leaving Jasper with only a daughter, the pretty Katherine.

As Jasper grew old and faced his own mortality, he realized that the beautiful estate of Larden had an uncertain fate unless he could persuade Katherine to marry well. Yet getting her to willingly marry advantageously appeared impossible. Katherine was already in love with—and secretly engaged to—a lowly yeoman named Jacob Blakeway. He was nothing but a farmer, owning a tiny parcel of land, his birth rendering him automatically beneath Jasper More's notice, but neither he nor Katherine cared. She loved him passionately, and she was intent upon marrying him.

Yet, in 17th-century England, love mattered little when land was at stake. Jasper and Richard cooked up a scheme that would keep Larden in the family once Jasper died. Richard's son, Samuel, would be forced to marry Katherine; Richard would then become the master of both estates, and ultimately, the entire inheritance would pass to Samuel. At least then, both Larden and Linley would remain the property of the More family. The alternative was unimaginable: Jacob Blakeway would inherit Larden if he married Katherine. It was simply unthinkable for a common oaf like him to possess such a vast tract of land.

Whether Katherine liked it or not, she had no choice. She was wed to Samuel in 1611, and they moved to Larden together to begin five years of a miserable and loveless marriage. Katherine and Samuel had both been forced into this decision: Katherine by her father and Samuel perhaps by greed or by pressure from his own father. At twenty-four, Katherine was six years older than her husband; Samuel, at seventeen, was little more than a boy himself.

Nonetheless, to the joy of the two scheming fathers, Katherine bore her first child to Samuel in 1612—a little girl named Elinor. Another child followed just a year later; this time, it was a boy, an heir who would inherit the combined estates of Larden and Linley. Katherine named him Jasper after her father. The third child, born in 1615, was a boy named Richard after Samuel's father—little Richard's grandfather. Or at least, so Samuel thought.

As Katherine continued to bring one child after the other into the world, suspicion began to grow in Samuel's heart. The marriage had been begrudgingly consummated, yet Samuel still spent most of his time in London on business, avoiding his wife in Larden as much as possible. What was more, he was noticing that his children bore far less resemblance to him than he'd expected.

By the time Katherine gave birth to her last child, Mary, in 1616, Samuel was quite certain that the children were not his own. In fact, they strongly resembled the man to whom Katherine had been betrothed: the yeoman Jacob Blakeway.

Seventeenth-century England saw adultery as a chargeable offense, and while Samuel knew that to separate from Katherine would be to endanger the estate, he could no longer bear to look at these children who appeared not to be his own. He sued Katherine for adultery in 1616, and immediately, she found herself in deep trouble. The law and its enforcers had little regard for women, especially women who had been found guilty of infidelity, and Katherine did not deny the adultery charge. She countered by trying to have her marriage to Samuel annulled, arguing that she had been legally betrothed to Jacob Blakeway, which would make her union with Samuel invalid.

But Katherine's promise with Jacob had been made in secret. There were no witnesses, and no one could validate her claim. Katherine was found guilty of adultery, as was Jacob Blakeway. Both faced insurmountable fines.

The poor little children, with four-year-old Elinor being the eldest at the time, found themselves caught in the middle of a legal battle as ugly as any modern-day divorce. Divorce itself was as yet unheard of then, but with Katherine accused of adultery, Samuel could have the marriage annulled. He did so, and in the process, he gained control of the children. If Katherine had hoped that her beloved Jacob would back her up in this difficult situation, she was entirely wrong. Jacob couldn't pay the fines. Instead, he simply disappeared, leaving Katherine all on her own.

Elinor, Jasper, Richard, and baby Mary were torn from Katherine's arms and sent to live with Samuel's parents. They were by no means happy to be caring for these illegitimate children, but Samuel was disgusted by their presence. Katherine herself was sent to live with her parents in London. The plans of the elder Richard and Jasper had backfired badly, for they now had no heirs at all since the children were not Samuel's but Jacob's. In fact, Richard Jr had no blood relation to Richard of Linley at all.

By 1620, when the *Mayflower* was preparing to set sail, Samuel had had enough. In his eyes, the children were nothing but a burden on his parents and an embarrassment to him. When he heard that anyone could book a space on the *Mayflower* to start a new life in America, Samuel realized that it was the perfect opportunity to ship the children far away so that they could never bother him again. He bought their passage across the Atlantic.

The children, who had no comprehension of why their parents no longer wanted them, found themselves being signed over into the care of complete strangers. Even worse, the children were abruptly separated and sent to live with different guardians. Only the two littlest, five-year-old Richard and four-year-old Mary, were able to stay together. William Brewster's heart went out to their plight, and he became the guardian of the two little ones.

Still, even in Brewster's care, the children—and every other passenger aboard the *Mayflower*—had no concept of the tribulation that lay before them. They were boarding their ships to escape hardship. Yet, the hardship they would endure in the next few years would far exceed what they had suffered before.

Chapter 4 – The Sad Fate of the Speedwell

Illustration II: Robert W. Weir's Embarkation of the Pilgrims.

For the Pilgrims, the trip to the Atlantic began at the port of Delfshaven.

The journey to Delfshaven was not a long one from Leiden: only about forty miles. Nonetheless, the Pilgrims spent the night of June 21st, 1620, in the port town where the *Speedwell* was docked. Many of their friends came from Amsterdam to spend the night with those who were departing for the New World, and perhaps for the first time since they gathered in William Brewster's manor back in England, the Scrooby Separatists were almost all together again.

Reverend John Robinson, though he had elected to stay behind in Leiden, had made the journey to Delfshaven to encourage his flock before their departure. The only non-Separatists to be boarding the *Speedwell* were Myles Standish and his family. All the others were Pilgrims, hoping for a new life.

It must have felt dreamlike and unreal to be sleeping in Delfshaven that night. For many of the Pilgrims, this would be their last night sleeping in a real bed, on solid ground, for many weeks. They were about to embark on a journey that few had ever attempted, and they were doing it in an unprecedented manner. Many of these Pilgrims had never even seen an artist's impressions of what America looked like. In fact, many modern-day Americans are more familiar with the surface of Mars than many of the Pilgrims would have been with the coast of America.

The atmosphere must have been one of both terror and excitement. The Pilgrims had hope, for the first time, to establish a settlement on their own terms, where their religion and culture could grow unhindered. But there was also so much to fear. They were truly adventuring entirely into the unknown.

After a near-sleepless night for many of the Pilgrims, the next morning began with final preparations to board the *Speedwell.* While, for many, that meant packing up the ship and getting her ready to leave, for Reverend Robinson and the other Pilgrims, their preparations were more spiritual in nature. With a crowd of Dutch onlookers curiously watching, Reverend Robinson preached a long sermon to the assembled Pilgrims. It must have been an emotional moment for him; even though he still planned to travel to America eventually, Robinson must have feared that he might never preach to these people again. After decades of ministering to them, from the secret meetings in Scrooby to the shores of Holland, Robinson finally had to say goodbye. It would be the last time he saw many of the people who were about to board the *Speedwell*, and it would be the last time many of them heard the beloved voice of their pastor, a voice that had guided them through so many trials and difficulties.

The crew of the *Speedwell* began to grow impatient as the sermon dragged on. The tide was going to turn against them if they didn't leave soon. Finally, the Pilgrims were told that it was time to go or they wouldn't be able to go that day at all. Reverend Robinson, overcome with fear and hope, fell to his knees and clutched at the hands of his flock. They, too, knelt down beside them, and all of them prayed together for the journey that they were about to begin.

Tears poured down Robinson's cheeks when he finally said his last farewells. The Pilgrims, pale-faced and nervous, made their way onto the *Speedwell.* Even the onlookers were in tears at the soulful scene before them.

It was to the sound of quiet weeping that the *Speedwell* at last drew away from the port and sailed out onto the English Channel.

* * * *

The journey to Southampton, where the *Speedwell* was due to rendezvous with the *Mayflower*, took about three days to complete. By July 25th, the *Speedwell* was sailing bravely into English waters once more. For many of the passengers, it had been as many as thirteen years since they had last set eyes on their English homeland. There were children among them who spoke English yet had never seen England before, and it must have been with jubilation that their parents could finally show them the land that they had once loved.

Yet, the jubilation didn't last long. Once the *Speedwell*'s passengers had disembarked and gone to see the *Mayflower* and its passengers, with some Pilgrims among them, they quickly found reason to be disgruntled. Not all of the *Speedwell*'s passengers had known that the Merchant Adventurers had sold passage aboard the *Mayflower* to non-Separatists. In fact, more of the *Mayflower*'s passengers were

Puritans or Anglicans than Separatists. There was great discontent among the Pilgrims over this issue, and Jones and Brewster had to smooth over some very ruffled feathers. The stark fact remained that without the money these people had paid to undertake the journey, the *Mayflower* wasn't going anywhere.

The Pilgrims were forced to accept this fact, but that didn't mean that they were happy about it. Even though many of the other passengers were simple farmers like themselves or even innocent children like the Mores, the Pilgrims still saw them as the "others" after having spent so many years in their tight-knit Separatist community. So, with considerable arrogance, they labeled the non-Separatist passengers "Strangers" and themselves as "Saints."

The next week saw the passengers spending even more of that money as they prepared to set sail. The *Mayflower* and the *Speedwell* needed to be loaded up, not only with travelers and what personal belongings they could fit aboard but also with enough food and water to supply them for many weeks. Their victuals would not only have to take them across the barren waste of the Atlantic Ocean but also last several months on the American shore itself. It could take months, if not even longer, to establish a self-sufficient colony there; food would be scarce until then. The Pilgrims brought all kinds of foods with them, as well as a handful of livestock–mainly sheep, goats, and poultry. There were also two dogs: a mastiff and a cheerful little spaniel. These animals would have to survive many long weeks in the bucking, rolling, dark hold of a ship before they would be able to stretch their legs or taste green grass again, and their suffering over the next part of the voyage is untold.

Many supplies, resources, and items of equipment had to be brought too. They needed all kinds of tools to construct homes on the new shore, and some of the building materials would have been impossible to find in America. They acquired hammers, nails, anvils, screws, and a gigantic jackscrew, a large device that could be adjusted in order to hold a load or steady a foundation. It was a small thing, but it would prove to be instrumental.

Fearing what they might face on the high seas and in the New World, the Pilgrims also brought with them some artillery pieces. The *Mayflower* wore guns, potentially for the first time, and they were a dark reminder of the fact that the Pilgrims weren't just peaceful travelers journeying to an untouched land. In reality, they were colonizers.

After spending a little over a week docked at Southampton, the *Mayflower*, the *Speedwell*, and their passengers—Saints and Strangers both—were finally ready to leave. At least, they were mostly ready. The *Speedwell* was already starting to give the Pilgrims cause for concern. She was forty-three years old, after all, and had seen much service. And although she had served her previous owners well, she was now beginning to show her age. She started taking on some water in Southampton's harbor. The local shipwrights did their best to patch her up, and the Pilgrims could only hope that she was ready for the long voyage.

On August 5th, 1620, the *Mayflower* and the *Speedwell* set sail together. For a Pilgrim standing upon the deck of one of those ships as they headed out into the British Channel, it must have been a moment of indescribable thrill and excitement, as well as great trepidation. With the wind straining the great sails, the hiss of the ocean along the bow, and the cries of the sailors as they swarmed over the rigging, this was a whole new adventure. They had left England in secret, smuggled in dark cargo holds; they left it again now on the deck of a ship they owned, in stunning summer daylight. The *Mayflower* held a reasonable load of about sixty-five passengers at that time.

Yet, that triumphant moment did not last long. Only a few days later, both ships had to turn back. The passengers had just begun to grow used to the rolling of the ships, and the open sea had just appeared at the end of the British Channel before them when disaster struck. The *Speedwell* began taking on water again. In fact, the leak was so severe that there was no possibility of making it across the Atlantic. She would have to return to England for repairs.

For Bradford, Brewster, and many other passengers aboard the *Speedwell*, this was a tragedy. The journey back to England would take time; repairing the *Speedwell* even more so. During this time, the passengers would still be eating victuals from the holds of the ships, precious food that could not be wasted. Perhaps Brewster and Bradford were already smelling disaster on the horizon. Brewster was responsible not only for his own family (his wife Mary and their two children, Love and Wrestling) but also for tiny Richard and Mary More—and, in a broader sense, for the entire community of hopeful people who had boarded the *Mayflower* and *Speedwell*.

Both ships changed direction and sailed into Dartmouth, arriving around August 15th, ten days into the voyage. Master Jones, Brewster, and Bradford had all hoped to be out on the Atlantic by now and making good progress to America, but their hopes were thoroughly dashed when Dartmouth's shipwrights told them that the repairs would take more than a week. The *Speedwell*'s timbers were pulling apart all over the hull, allowing so much water into the ship that it could ruin her cargo and even sink the ship.

For nine long days, the *Speedwell* and the *Mayflower* lay at anchor. For all that time, the passengers were still living in their bunks. "Our victuals will be half eaten up, I think, before we go from the coast of England," William Bradford wrote dolefully in his journal. Their situation was growing more and more perilous.

Finally, on August 24th—more than a month since the *Speedwell* had set sail from Delfshaven; the Pilgrims had hoped to be more than halfway across the sea by that time— Dartmouth's shipwrights at last finished their repairs. Once again, the *Speedwell* and the *Mayflower* left England and sailed down the British Channel toward open waters.

And after several days, it seemed at last that they were making good progress. The green strip of Land's End, located on the Penwith Peninsula in Cornwall, England, faded behind the ships; the wind drove them out upon the churning waves, and with every mile that slipped past under the speeding hulls, the Pilgrims drew nearer to the land that they had long dreamed of. The *Speedwell*'s creaking old timbers were holding together, if barely. The *Mayflower* was skimming along, with Master Jones at the helm, enjoying the feeling of sailing his own ship across the open ocean. For the first time, many of the passengers experienced the feeling of being surrounded by nothing but glittering miles of water in all directions. Hope rose among the passengers, and they spoke of the new world they were about to experience.

But their trials with the *Speedwell* were not over yet. Three hundred miles out on the open sea, she started leaking again.

This was disastrous. They had already traveled so far. Jones was acutely aware that time was slipping inexorably past and that the foul storms of fall were nearly upon them. They needed to get to America quickly before the summer was spent. But the *Speedwell* was endangering the lives of everyone on board. There was no other choice. Once again, brokenhearted, the *Mayflower* and the *Speedwell* had to turn back. They sailed into the nearest English port, one that would ultimately lend its name to the colony the Pilgrims would establish: Plymouth.

It was September by the time both ships sailed wearily into the harbor at Plymouth, and they were carrying a cargo of deeply disheartened passengers and crew. The Pilgrims had been unhappy at the prospect of a five-week voyage across the Atlantic in the company of the Strangers; they had now been at sea with them for a month already, and they hadn't even left England yet. The berths on the ships were cramped and crowded, the food was dry, and nothing and no one was fresh. Discontent was spreading like a plague, as was the bad blood between the Saints and Strangers. Bradford went as far as suspecting the captain of the *Speedwell* of sabotage. While it seems unlikely that any captain would willingly sign up to cross the Atlantic and then sabotage his ship, especially three hundred miles out to sea, Bradford made a good point in that the *Speedwell* had served many of her masters well since she'd been recommissioned.

Still, it would appear that the more logical explanation for the *Speedwell*'s troubles was that recommissioning. When she left the English navy, the *Speedwell* was refitted with new and far too large of sails in order to make her a faster merchant vessel. She ended up carrying far too much sail, however, and her aging timbers simply couldn't take the strain. They were pulling apart, and the shipwrights at Plymouth had to give the Pilgrims and Merchant Adventurers some very bad news. The *Speedwell* was unseaworthy. She wouldn't be making the trip across the Atlantic, no matter how much money they spent trying to repair her.

Brewster, Bradford, Weston, and everyone else involved in the voyage were absolutely horrified. It seemed as though the entire mission was thoroughly doomed. They had already spent a small fortune buying and repairing the *Speedwell*; the summer was already spent, and at this rate, they would reach America right before winter. There would be little time to establish crops, build homes, and do all the other necessary things in order to survive in a whole new continent. In fact, the Pilgrims came perilously close to abandoning their journey entirely. We may never have known the name of the *Mayflower*, and their failure might have faded into the oblivion of history.

But the Pilgrims were determined. They still fervently believed that they were destined to establish their colony in America and that it was God's will for them to leave Europe behind and build a new settlement just for Separatists. The Merchant Adventurers, too, had invested far too much money in this venture to simply abandon it now. People had paid for their passage across the Atlantic, and they were going to get that passage, come hell or high water. In the next few weeks, the travelers would experience some form of both.

Led by Brewster, Bradford, and Jones, the Pilgrims realized that try as they might, they couldn't all go to America on the *Mayflower*. There just wasn't any room; she was comfortably at capacity with sixty-five passengers aboard her already. The Merchant Adventurers, obviously, turned down the notion of leaving any of the paying passengers behind. As a result, some of the Pilgrims had no choice but to turn back and return to Leiden, their hopes dashed and deep disappointment in their hearts. We don't know how exactly it was decided which Pilgrims would go and which would stay. We do know that many children and women, including several pregnant women, would still stay aboard the ship; most families were kept together, at least in the Separatist community.

Still, it was with a sorrowful heart that many Pilgrims had to give up on their dreams—at least for the time being—and go back to Holland with their tails between their legs. Only twenty of the *Speedwell*'s Pilgrim passengers could make their way aboard the *Mayflower*. By the time all of the paying passengers and the crew were crammed on board alongside the "Saints," the *Mayflower* was far beyond her capacity, even before they added all the extra victuals that the *Speedwell* had been carrying.

The gallant little ship had 102 passengers on board—of which only a few were Pilgrims (41 men and their families)—by the time they were finished, along with all the supplies and animals they needed to keep them alive across the Atlantic and establish a new home on that distant shore. William Bradford and William Brewster, along with their families, were among them; so were John Carver and Catherine, who had seven-year-old Jasper More in their charge. Perhaps he was a substitute for the children they had wanted but who had not survived back in Leiden.

And even when the last preparations were made, the *Mayflower* still lay at anchor for one endless week. A terrible calm had fallen upon Plymouth; hardly a breath of wind stirred, and the *Mayflower* barely rocked on the mirror-smooth surface of the harbor. The days must have slipped by with interminable slowness as the passengers waited, their food ever dwindling, the winter coming ever closer. But finally, finally, on September 16th, 1620, a great wind rose up and tugged at the sails of the *Mayflower*.

As the little ship headed at last out of Plymouth, the mood on board must have been very different compared to the festive air that had surrounded the two ships when they first set sail from Southampton. The Pilgrims had hoped to be treading upon American soil already; now, they were only just setting off from England, bereft of their ship, their money, many of their resources, and even much of their community. Everything was going to be much harder now, not least because they were sailing in the fall, a time when the seas grew ever more dangerous.

If there was any hope aboard that ship at that time, it must have been very subdued. In fear and trembling, the *Mayflower*'s passengers waited silently as the little ship slid quietly onto the open sea at last.

Chapter 5 – Tossed by the Storms

Illustration III: After the Storm *by William Bradford (1861).*

Our story has now taken us back to Master Christopher Jones as he clung desperately to the helm of the *Mayflower* as she courageously butted her way up a mountain of turbulent water. Flecked with spray, the wave towered up into the storm-churned sky, robbed of the stars that were Jones's navigation. Instead, it boiled with clouds, torn apart by a great crack of lightning that ran across the face of the firmament.

The lightning illuminated the terrified faces of the sailors struggling to tame the sails, keeping them bound tightly to the masts, lest the wind take them and run the ship off the very edge of the world.

The *Mayflower* pitched violently on the crest of the wave. She sped down the tossing slope of water, her timbers squealing with the force of her speed. Jones had lashed himself to the helm; the ropes cut into his hands as the *Mayflower* thundered on. She reached the trough of the wave with a bone-shattering thud. A torrent of water washed over the deck, knee-deep and irresistible; Jones only just kept his footing as he clung to the helm.

When he regained his balance and looked up, he saw disaster had come upon them. There was a deafening crack, but this time, it wasn't lightning. It was the mainmast. It had been appallingly damaged, a terrible crack running across the great timber, and the tip of it swayed dramatically in the howling wind. (It is entirely possible that this could have been a main beam.)

But there was no time to worry about the mainmast now, even though Jones knew they'd be adrift and starving on the open sea without it. Another wave was coming—a hundred-foot monster bent on devouring the tiny ship that dared stand against it.

Jones braced himself, and the *Mayflower* once again began her perilous ascent.

* * * *

Jones had known that they were inviting disaster when they set sail from Plymouth Harbor on September 16th, 1620. Summer was the time for sailing, and thanks to the *Speedwell*'s shenanigans, summer had long since passed.

It was into the deadly fall winds that the *Mayflower* sailed, and Jones knew as they left the harbor that the strong wind that drove her now so steadily toward her destination would soon change and become the deadly nor'easter that brought howling storms crashing across the Atlantic.

Still, after leaving Plymouth, the travelers were blessed with nearly five weeks of smooth sailing. For thirty-three days, the passengers of the *Mayflower* only had the usual tribulations to contend with.

The *Mayflower* had been pretty cramped even before the *Speedwell* had had to transfer many of her passengers aboard it. In fact, with sixty-five passengers on board, the *Mayflower* had been filled to the brim. Now, she was uncomfortably full, carrying 102 passengers and a crew of 37. The ship herself was capable of carrying the weight, but relations between the passengers were considerably more strained.

The Saints and Strangers were now crammed almost shoulder to shoulder in tiny living spaces. In the tiny space called the gun decks, which were between the upper deck and the cargo hold, makeshift berths had been made for the passengers. The gun decks had a ceiling that was only five feet high. All but the shortest of people and the smallest of children couldn't even stand up straight in their rooms. Roaming around the deck was not exactly forbidden, but it was generally discouraged by the sailors, who were more accustomed to hauling wool and wine than human beings—landlubbers—who would bumble around and get in their way. There were also many fears that the tossing waves would prove too much for the Pilgrims and that someone would be thrown overboard. It was a fear that would later be dramatically justified. As a result, most of the passengers spent almost every single moment of those sixty-six days at sea in their tiny, cramped living quarters.

The entire area allocated to the passengers was 1,600 square feet: half the size of most modern-day American homes. The space was unbearably tight. To make matters worse, there was no privacy. Couples, single people, and entire families were crammed in there together, and there were no rooms. In a desperate attempt at some semblance of privacy, some passengers tried to made dividers with bits of wood or curtains with whatever fabric they had on hand.

These people had been living in these appalling conditions ever since Delfshaven back in July. However, when they were in port waiting for the *Speedwell* to be repaired, at least there was the chance of some fresh food, whether it was bread, dairy products, or perhaps even fruit or vegetables. Here on the open sea, there was no chance of that. Only preserved meats and hardtack biscuits could survive such a long voyage. Even water would no longer be potable after several weeks at sea; instead, men, women, children, and infants were forced to drink beer. The alcohol was little help for the inevitable dehydration that soon set in. The beer caused throbbing headaches, and on top of that, there was the strength-sapping scurvy from which many soon began to suffer. The beer also did not help with the seasickness.

Most of these people weren't used to sailing at all either. In fact, of every living soul aboard the *Mayflower*, only one had ever been to the New World. Stephen Hopkins had gone to Jamestown in earlier years, leaving his first wife back in England. When she passed away, he returned to the Old World and married a new wife: Elizabeth. She had given him three children and was copiously pregnant with a fourth when they boarded the *Mayflower*. While Stephen was accustomed to these conditions and long voyages, Elizabeth was not. It must have been almost intolerable for her, a heavily pregnant woman in such a tight space, trying to keep three little kids entertained as the long days slipped slowly by.

Elizabeth and Stephen had hoped that she would bring forth their next child in the New World. If things had gone according to plan, they would have been in America for almost two months already. Instead, she went into labor on board that ship—that crowded, dirty ship, where there was no privacy and no room. Assisted by Dr. Samuel Fuller, a Separatist physician and one of the Pilgrims, Elizabeth gave birth to a healthy little boy. His parents aptly named him Oceanus.

America was growing closer. Everyone aboard the *Mayflower* was starting to feel more and more optimistic; the successful birth of a new life, the shimmering beauty of the seas, and the knowledge that the New World was just days away were all heady stuff. But in mid-October, things changed for the worse.

A deadly northeasterly wind began to blow, howling the ominous tidings of approaching disaster. Soon, the beautiful blue sky and the shimmering blue sea were gone, replaced by turbulent clouds and tossing gray waves that grew higher and higher with every gust of wind.

For the next month, the *Mayflower* was buffeted relentlessly by one devastating storm after the other. On deck, Master Jones and the crew suffered as they were washed this way and that, thrown around like rag dolls on the pitching surface of the ship. But things were no better below. As the ship climbed one one-hundred-foot swell after the other, the passengers were thrown all over the gun decks while panicking animals squealed in the hold below. Children screamed, babies cried, women clung desperately to their husbands, husbands clung desperately to their families, and the lonely held on to whatever was closest.

William Bradford would describe that month of awful storms as "a long beating at sea." It certainly felt as though the passengers were being pummeled. Their belongings would have skidded helplessly across the floor of the hold while people and things smashed into one another, bruising one another. The ship creaked alarmingly all around them as though at any moment she might fly to pieces and drown them all. Seasickness was prevalent, and it would have made the stench in the hold, which was already a fog of compressed humanity, grow all the more dreadful.

When the storms were at their peak, tossing great mountains of water over the ship, there was no way to keep anything dry, even within the hold. Sheets of water gushed down over the passengers, drenching everyone and everything they owned. For Oceanus, it was a baptism in seawater; for the other children, it was a dark and terrifying ordeal as they clung to their families, the floor pitching under them, the darkness absolute, and great waves of water washing over them. Everything was soaked—the food, the people, the animals, and even the bedding.

It was in one of these storms that the *Mayflower* suffered her first and only loss of life during the voyage. Dr. Samuel Fuller's servant, a youth named William Butten, died in the midst of one of the storms. It's unclear what took Butten's life, but Bradford described it as a "grievous disease." Whatever the case, Butten became the first *Mayflower* passenger to die. As soon as it was safe to do so, he was buried at sea, and his body sank down into the Atlantic. It must have been a sober moment for all the passengers. Land was nowhere in sight, and it may have felt as though they would all inevitably share Butten's fate.

John Howland, another indentured servant (this time to John Carver), was another man who nearly met his end aboard the *Mayflower* during a storm. If it wasn't for the quick thinking of another sailor, he might have joined Butten at the bottom of the sea.

* * *

Even though Howland was an indentured servant, he was an educated man, and in later years, he would serve as an important secretary and assistant to John Carver. Born in England during the 1590s—likely in 1592—Howland may have become a servant to Carver in exchange for passage over the Atlantic.

Religious controversy was nothing new to Howland's family. Both of his brothers were Quakers, which was part of an even more radical Reformation sect that existed upon the very fringe of Christianity's traditional definitions. Howland himself, however, was a Separatist, and it seemed that servitude was a price he was more than willing to pay in order to be given the chance of a new life in a new world where he could live out the faith in which he so passionately believed.

It appears that Howland's duties as a servant were mostly bookish ones. He had brought little onto the *Mayflower* other than his Bible and some commentaries, and he would help John Carver with making notes and keeping records. Yet, even he couldn't bear the confinement of the gun decks. The unbearably close space, the stench of vomit, the unrelenting crush of people—Howland couldn't take it anymore. In the midst of a crashing storm, he pushed past the other passengers and walked out onto the deck.

That breath of fresh air must have been glorious, with no stench and no vomit, just the cool, clean spray and the refreshing rush of rain in his face. But Howland's relief didn't last long. In moments, he would find out why the captain had confined the passengers to the gun decks.

With the captain striving valiantly to control the bucking, tossing *Mayflower* on the unrelenting waves, every strong arm on the ship was needed to bail water and perform the thousand other duties necessary for everyone aboard to survive. The cracked mainmast tossed in the howling wind, the wet and slippery deck heaved underneath the feet of the crew and passengers, and screams of panic came from below deck as the passengers were drenched with rain and seawater.

John Howland was a bookish landlubber, and he had never seen the open sea before they'd left the British Channel more than a month ago. Now, however, he was forced to find his sea legs fast. The roaring waves towered over the *Mayflower*, dwarfing both the ship and everyone aboard. The whole world seemed upside down and inside out, with lightning crackling from one side of the sky to the other and spray and rain making the air feel almost as wet as the ocean herself.

A mighty swell rose over the deck of the hapless ship. There were cries of alarm, but there was no way John Howland could have escaped what was coming next. His uneducated limbs couldn't keep him upright even on a moderate swell, let alone the hundred-foot monsters the *Mayflower* was bravely climbing. The next thing he knew, a wall of water was rushing toward him. It struck his limbs with breathtaking force, and Howland knew a moment of appalling terror as he was borne off his feet, tossed helplessly on the cascade of rushing water, and then cast overboard.

It is difficult to imagine, let alone describe, the sheer terror Howland must have felt as he tumbled into the dark ocean. The *Mayflower* had been an oasis of civilization, the only proof that other humans even existed, for the many weeks that Howland and the other passengers had been crossing the open sea. Week upon week had slipped past with no sign of any other people, no contact with the rest of the world; there had just been the sea and the ship that had become their home. And now, Howland was looking up at her, at the rough timbers that creaked and whined as they were thrown hither and thither on the waters, and she was his last hope.

The roiling sea was upon him, grasping him, throwing him down into the utter darkness. Water filled his ears, reached for his lungs; noise and pressure crushed him further and further down toward the deep and whatever lay therein. With burning lungs and limbs stiffened by the unspeakable cold, Howland must have felt absolutely helpless—and then his flailing, outstretched hand found something rough and firm. A rope. It was a trailing topsail halyard that had fallen into the sea, and by sheer luck, his desperate hand had grasped it.

Still, with all the chaos on deck, it took several moments for the crew to notice that Howland was missing in the first place. For a few moments that must have felt like an eternity, Howland was towed behind the speeding, bucking *Mayflower*. He held on grimly, knowing that the rough halyard was all that stood between him and certain death. And all the while, he was sinking deeper and deeper, the flickering light of the storm growing fainter and fainter above him. He sank as many as twelve feet, and both his grip and his hope were growing feeble when, finally, there was a great tug on the halyard. A quick-thinking crew member had noticed that something was dragging on the rope and started pulling.

With a mighty effort from the crew, Howland's head was at last lifted above the water, and he clung on to the halyard–tossed all the while in the ocean, slammed at times against the rough timbers of the *Mayflower* herself–as continued efforts were made to raise him. At last, a boat hook was thrown to him, and Howland was pulled from the deadly clutches of the ocean to the comparative safety of the *Mayflower*'s deck.

The ordeal had been terrifying, but Howland was mostly unharmed. He was soaked to the skin, exhausted, and frightened to his very bones, but he was alive, and he would go on to become one of Plymouth Colony's most important figures.

Amazingly, no one else fell overboard during the devastating storms through which the *Mayflower* so suffered. And apart from the luckless William Butten, there were no deaths.

* * * *

Even when the worst of the storms had passed, Master Jones knew that the danger was still intense. It was with grim dismay that he showed the leaders of the Pilgrims, including William Bradford, the extent of the damage to the *Mayflower*'s mainmast.

Bradford, Brewster, and the other Pilgrims felt both helpless and terrified as Master Jones pointed out the terrible crack. The *Mayflower*'s mainmast was her principal method of propulsion. As it was now, it would never be able to take the strain of the wind filling the mainsail, meaning there would be no way for the *Mayflower* to continue her journey to America.

To have come so far and survived so much to be crippled for want of a mainmast–it was too heartbreaking for words. What was worse, Jones wasn't sure where exactly they were at that point. The winds and storms had driven them wildly off course, pushing them much farther north than they had planned, and provisions were running low. It was almost November by then; the passengers had been aboard the ship since leaving Delfshaven in July, and they were exhausted and hungry.

Many of them had grown sick thanks to the cold and wet conditions inside the *Mayflower*'s hold.

Now, without a mainsail, even arriving at any form of land would be impossible. Jones and the others had to face an utterly appalling fate: drifting helplessly on the open ocean until madness or thirst killed them all.

In fact, that would have been the end of the *Mayflower*'s story had it not been for the fact that one enterprising colonist had found room in the hold for a tool that many others would have considered a luxury. This man—whom history does not name—knew that building a home in the New World would be challenging enough, so he brought a jackscrew with him: a large tool that could be used for adjusting the foundation of a home.

In a pinch, though, it could also be used to hold the ruined mainmast together. The colonist brought it out, and the men exacted a tenuous repair. It was unorthodox, sure enough, but at least the *Mayflower*'s mainsail could be unfurled once more and billow in the rising wind, allowing her to propel the passengers once again toward their destination.

After all that they had survived, it must have been an emotional moment to see the mainsail once again fill up with wind. The hearts of the men watching must have swelled and lifted just as that expanse of white canvas did.

The storms had subsided at last. Bradford had managed to save his diary despite the wet conditions below deck. He had been writing in it for nearly four months now, and he wrote his first November entry with hope in his heart.

Yet, that hope began to wear thin for everyone on board as one fair day after the other passed, with the *Mayflower* sailing ever on and with no sight of land. The voyage should have taken five weeks. More than seven weeks had already passed, and yet every morning, the Pilgrims rose and saw nothing but rippling ocean in every direction.

Days slipped past. The *Mayflower* butted on resolutely. Master Jones doubted his own navigation skills, wondering if he was reading the stars correctly. At night, silence and darkness spread in all directions, the stars reflecting in the water, making it feel as if the ship was floating in a sphere of endless sky.

Hope was waning in the *Mayflower*'s hold when the glorious cry rang at last through the crisp, still air: "Land ho!"

It was daybreak on the morning of November 19th, 1620, more than three months after the *Speedwell* had first left Delfshaven with those hopeful Pilgrims on board. Their number had been thinned by the loss of the *Speedwell*, and they were all hungry and cold and battered as they ventured on deck in the slowly growing morning light. But hope rose in them all as their eyes finally rested on the most blessed sight any of them had ever seen.

The sun was rising, not over rippling ocean but over solid land.

* * * *

If the Pilgrims believed that their voyage was at an end at last when they finally set eyes on land once more, they were sadly disappointed.

As the *Mayflower* drew nearer to the green strip of land that beckoned to them from the horizon, Master Jones's suspicions were confirmed. They had reached North America, all right, but there was no sign of the Hudson River's mouth, the place the Pilgrims had legally claimed and the only part of the continent to which they had any right in the eyes of Europe.

Instead, the Pilgrims were looking at modern-day Cape Cod, hundreds of miles northeast from the Hudson River.

Although they could see land at last, they had no permission to reach it and feel solid ground beneath one's feet and see real trees and birds and animals and dirt and grass and rocks again—it must have been unbearable. But the *Mayflower*'s passengers felt that they had to honor the agreement they had made with King James, not only to avoid persecution but also to appease the Merchant Adventurers, who had already put a considerable amount of money into this venture and would be highly disgusted to discover that the ship had failed to reach its intended destination and landed on some arbitrary stretch of the American coast instead.

Despite the fact that the nor'easter was still blowing the *Mayflower* ever farther north, Master Jones had no choice but to prolong the terrible voyage. He swung the *Mayflower*'s nose to the south, keeping the land ever on his right, and began to attempt a laborious trek along two hundred miles of unexplored coastline, hoping to find the Hudson River.

The attempt proved absolutely futile. Not only was Cape Cod unmapped, but it was also littered with rocks, and every fathom that the *Mayflower* sailed risked shattering her tired hull on some unseen rock. With provisions running low, many of the passengers sick or starving or simply exhausted by being at sea in those cramped conditions for so long, and the risk of a shipwreck rising with every rock that grated at the bottom of the *Mayflower*'s hull, Master Jones and the other leaders decided that enough was enough. They had risked their lives for long enough, and they would risk them no further. The captain turned the *Mayflower* around and headed back to the last useful bay they had passed.

And so, finally, on November 21st, 1620—122 days after people like Myles Standish, John Carver, and William Brewster had first boarded the *Speedwell* at Delfshaven—the *Mayflower* finally sailed into a small bay and lay at anchor at last. Its passengers gazed out upon solid ground again, and it was a beautiful land, with tall trees all decked out in their autumn colors, soft golden-green hills rising up to meet the horizon, and the bay gleaming like a mirror between the warm and verdant arms of the trees.

The bay would ultimately become known as Provincetown, Massachusetts. But at that moment, it was to the Pilgrims' eyes a complete wilderness.

Before the Pilgrims could land, however, there was one enormous problem to be dealt with. That was the fact that they had been assigned a specific tract of land near the Hudson River. Never mind the fact that the land had never belonged to King James in the first place—it was home to the people who had lived there for centuries. But in the Pilgrims' eyes, they rightfully owned a specific part of the North American continent. Now, though, they found themselves 220 miles northeast of the Hudson's mouth. They were far outside the boundaries of the land they had been given.

But sailing southward wasn't an option. Neither was returning home with their tails between their legs; they had already set sail too late, and they would never survive the storms of the return trip even if they had had enough provisions to make it. They were in America now, and they would have to make a home for themselves here in this bay or die trying.

Still, that left them outside of the boundaries of any European government, a terrifying thought to the order-loving Separatists. There were no laws here, no means of enforcing their religious freedom, no ways of establishing the hierarchy that had been agreed upon back in the civilization of the Old World.

The new colony hadn't even been established yet, and it was already teetering upon the brink of anarchy. There was no way of contacting King James to modify their agreement. There was no one in the world they could consult except the people upon that very ship.

For that reason, it was necessary to think of a whole new system of government and do something that had never been done before. And thus, the Mayflower Compact was born.

Chapter 6 – The First Winter

Illustration IV: William Halsall's The Mayflower in Plymouth Harbor.

During the long journey across the angry ocean, there had been comparative peace between the Saints, the Strangers, and the crew. Even though some of the passengers, like John Howland, had resented the fact that the crew was more or less forcing them to stay below deck, there had been no time for any real conflict. The passengers had been too focused on survival to argue among themselves, and any kind of interpersonal grievance had seemed trivial compared with the terrifying reality of the lurching ship and the unending sea.

But hardly had the *Mayflower* dropped anchor in Provincetown Harbor than trouble began to brew among the passengers. The Saints were still wholly focused on their original goal of establishing an entirely Separatist colony here in the New World, a "New Israel," as Pastor Robinson had called it back in Leiden. That was the whole purpose of their voyage. In their eyes, unless they could build a country upon Separatist principles, they had suffered the long voyage for nothing.

The Strangers, unsurprisingly, found the Saints' attitudes considerably stifling. Not only were the Saints desperate for the Strangers to conform to their vision of what their new colony would be, but they also considered themselves to be more important than the Strangers, as they had planned and organized the mission.

Friction rose sharply as the *Mayflower* rested in Provincetown Harbor, and tensions began to boil over. To make matters worse, now that they were technically outside of the English Crown's territory, it seemed that no one could exercise any kind of authority over the mutinous passengers, whose complaints and angry speeches were stirring up more and more discontent.

Carver and Brewster were both deeply worried about what was going on. Robinson had entrusted the leadership of the Pilgrims during the voyage to them, and they feared that here, on the very doorstep of the new land they intended to inhabit, they were about to be robbed of their hopes and dreams. Drastic action would have to be taken if the Pilgrims were going to live out their dream of a Separatist colony. Something unprecedented would have to be done. Together, the Pilgrim leaders decided to draw up a document unlike any other: the Mayflower Compact.

For most people of the Old World, the very idea of constructing a contract of self-government, a legal document for the government of an entire colony, would have been absolutely outrageous. But for Brewster, it was old news. He had helped to draft vital documents for the foundation of the Separatist church back in England, and the compact was based upon those documents, albeit with one major difference: the Mayflower Compact swore allegiance to King James I.

Brewster and Carver likely worked together on composing the compact, although, to this day, it's uncertain who authored this groundbreaking document. While its very first lines told of how the colonists promised to stay loyal to the English king, it has also been considered one of the earliest attempts at democracy and the foundation of the Constitution of the United States of America, which would follow many years later. Never before had self-government been attempted in a North American colony.

The Mayflower Compact, as recorded by William Bradford, was a short document, hastily composed and to the point. In fact, it is little more than a couple of paragraphs, but it laid the foundation for one of the United States' earliest colonies. In it, the Pilgrims promised to create and abide by "just and equal" laws for the benefit of everyone in the colony. While "justice" and "equality" sounds outrageously inaccurate to modern ears, considering that neither the women nor the Strangers were given any say in the contents of the compact, the document did save the colony from slipping into total anarchy. The compact also promised that the Pilgrims would create one society rather than separating the Saints and the Strangers.

The compact was enforced by the looming presence of Myles Standish, who may have been the only non-Separatist to sign the document. In all, forty-one men signed the Mayflower Compact. John Carver was the first, Bradford the second, and Brewster was the third. Samuel Fuller was there too, as was John Howland.

During the signing of the compact, the men also elected a governor for the colony. This turned out to be John Carver. He had likely been instrumental in composing the Mayflower Compact, had helped to finance the mission, and had been one of the first people to dare to believe in the idea that an ordinary group of people could make it to the New World. What was more, he'd always been a strong leader as a deacon in the church, and the other Pilgrims looked up to him.

It was unorthodox, but it worked. While disunion and occasional squabbles would continue to plague the Saints and Strangers throughout the long winter that would follow, the Mayflower Compact survived as the governing document of the colony for more than seven decades.

* * * *

The Mayflower Compact secured a tenuous peace among the passengers. This must have been much to the relief of Master Jones; although he had no part in constructing the compact and didn't sign it, he must have been worried about the rebellious mood aboard the *Mayflower*. Any captain fears mutiny.

Even though many of the Strangers still muttered in discontent, understandably so considering they had been given no say in the matter, the passengers were nonetheless able to turn their attention to another looming challenge: surviving the oncoming winter.

It was late November by this time, and a New England winter was setting in across the bay where the *Mayflower* lay at anchor. A bitter cold assailed the passengers as they waited in their berths. Their provisions, which had already been lower than they would have liked when they left Plymouth Harbor behind, were dwindling rapidly. They had hoped to have arrived in the New World by the end of August, with plenty of time to plant a few crops that would get them through the winter. But the ground, now, was growing cold and unyielding.

There was precious little water left aboard the *Mayflower* too, and everyone was growing tired and dehydrated from the beer. There wasn't time for dissent. It was time to focus on survival.

The day after the Mayflower Compact was signed, everyone aboard the *Mayflower* followed the Separatists' example and took a day of rest; after all, it was a Sunday. The Separatists prayed desperately that, somehow, their crazy plan would work. They believed that it was God's power alone that had brought them across that treacherous ocean, and indeed, Master Jones would have agreed that surviving the journey had been miraculous. Now, however, they knew they faced even greater tribulation. Little could they have imagined the hardship they were about to experience.

On November 23rd, 1620, the Pilgrims finally left the *Mayflower* behind and ventured onto the shore of the New World. What a blessed relief it must have been to set foot once more upon dry land! And after the bucking, wobbling, crowded, dark, and dingy gun decks of the *Mayflower*, that first breath of clean air, standing on sturdy ground, must have been an inexpressible delight. The verdant colors of the trees, the brilliance of the clear sky...it was all so good and so beautiful. William Bradford described a scene of joy and relief in his journal. The Pilgrims were cold, tired, and close to starving, all of them suffering from sickness, dehydration, and malnourishment, but they had finally reached a free land. Every hill and tree, every valley and bay they set eyes on was beyond the reach of the king who had made their lives so difficult. They could be free at last now, even if they were free only to die.

Their feeble but fervent joy did not last long. Even though everyone was exhausted and sickly, there was work to be done if they had any hope of surviving the winter that lay ahead.

The crew quickly got to work putting together a draft boat that had been taken apart back in England for storage in the *Mayflower*'s cargo hold. Known as a shallop, she was fairly small, but she would carry a few sailors or fishermen where they wanted to go. The shallop was a poor substitute for the *Speedwell*, which would have stayed behind with the colonists, but at least she was something–and she would prove instrumental in finding the bay where they would ultimately establish their colony.

Rebuilding the shallop would take time, however, and time was a luxury that the colonists did not have. Every breeze that blew was colder and tore more and more brown leaves from the trees. There was not yet snow, but hard frosts came in the night, cold enough to freeze the earth. This made everything worse, as little aboard the *Mayflower*, including clothes and bedding, had had a chance to dry out after being drenched during the storms. Finding a place to build homes would be imperative to the survival of the colony, and although the area immediately surrounding the bay was beautiful, it was too rocky and hilly for the colonists to build there.

While they were waiting for the shallop to be rebuilt, the colonists selected a group of explorers—led, of course, by Myles Standish—to venture deeper inland and search for a place where they could plant crops, build homes, and establish the lives they had so long dreamed of.

In early December, Standish and a small group of men set out. The jubilation of their arrival in the New World had given away to a quietly throbbing desperation. The men in that expedition had families waiting aboard the *Mayflower*; they had seen their wives suffer, watched their children weep for week upon terrifying week across that ocean. Their children were emaciated. Their wives were depressed. They had promised them that life would be better out here, but so far, they had gone from poverty and oppression to starvation and danger. They were desperate to help their families.

As they ventured across the countryside, heading through the woods and up and down the hills, the party grew desperate in another way too. There was precious little water left on the *Mayflower*, and the bay in which she now lay was salty. They had taken nothing with them except for a bottle of liquor. It did nothing to slake their thirst as they went onward, and they had been dehydrated enough to start with; what was more, these men had had little exercise in all those weeks at sea, and weakness soon began to overcome them.

They were starting to grow feeble with cold and thirst when they finally found it: the first freshwater spring that the Pilgrims would discover in the New World. It was just a seep of fresh water from the ground, but to those men, it was life. At last, for the first time in weeks, they could kneel down and cup their hands around that abundant freshness and drink and drink and drink until their thirst was slaked at last.

Moving onward, refreshed by their first good drink of water in weeks, the group came across their first sign of civilization: a grave. They had stumbled upon a burial ground belonging to the Native Americans in that area.

From the beginning, the Pilgrims had decided that they would avoid conflict with the indigenous peoples at all costs. For one thing, they weren't warriors; they didn't stand a chance against a group of angry Native Americans defending their homes. For another, they hoped to evangelize the Native Americans, not murder them. More than that, the Pilgrims were different from the Jamestown colonists in that they had not come to the New World for money. They weren't there to plunder the locals and murder anyone who stood in their way of colonizing the New World. Instead, these people were refugees, fleeing from a regime that didn't allow them to live the way they wanted. They were invading the homes of these Native Americans because they no longer had homes to call their own.

Accordingly, Standish and the others hoped to barter with the Native Americans for food and other goods, and they'd brought along some beads, which had historically been successful in trading, to exchange for the things they needed. But desperation and fear now clouded their earlier hopes. When they came upon the grave, they began to dig. No one knows what exactly they hoped to find, but when they uncovered a bow and arrows, it brought home to them the fact that these were people who would fight to protect their homelands. Standish stopped the men, realizing how disgusting the act of disturbing this grave would be. They covered it over with earth again but not before stumbling upon a stash of something that would be more valuable at that moment to the colonists than any amount of gold or jewels: corn.

Although corn was relatively unknown to these English farmers at the time, they knew from reports by other colonists that corn was a key crop in the New World. Native Americans had been growing it there for centuries upon centuries. Growing it would ensure the colonists' survival, and the Pilgrims were desperate.

It's unclear whether they didn't know or just didn't care that the corn hadn't been buried there to be dug up and used again later. It was a sacrificial offering, buried with the dead in order to help them in the afterlife. Standish and the others may have thought that they were just stealing, but in reality, they were desecrating something sacred in the eyes of the native people. Their actions that day would be similar to setting set fire to a church. The Pilgrims did hope, however, that they would be able to find the natives and repay them for the corn they had taken.

After some time, Standish's party came upon a Native American village. The indigenous people of the area–the Nauset–were semi-nomadic, moving from one established village to the other with the seasons. The village that Standish found was completely empty, either because the Nauset had moved southward for the winter or because the terrified inhabitants were hiding from these armed men. Once again, the Pilgrims took several items from the Nausets' homes. They had intended to leave beads behind to trade instead of just stealing, but hunger and desperation made them forget their good intentions toward anyone other than themselves, and so, they simply took what they wanted and carried it back toward the *Mayflower*.

When they returned, at least one piece of good news greeted them. Firstly, the shallop was nearly done, and secondly, another baby had been born in the *Mayflower*'s gun decks. Susanna White, the wife of William White, had hoped that she would have been safely installed in a cozy little cottage by the time her child was born. Instead, she brought him into the world in the filthy berth with no privacy or hygiene.

The little boy was named Peregrine, and he was the first Pilgrim child to be born in the New World and among the first English children born in North America. His elder brother, Resolved, was one of the children who had journeyed to the New World on the *Mayflower*. It is difficult to imagine the desperation and fear that Susanna White must have felt as she wrapped her newborn child in rags. Her boy had been born free, unlike little Resolved, free to worship in whatever way he pleased. But the future was so uncertain, the bitter winter drawing so near, and the baby's plaintive cries split the air with a note piercing enough to break any mother's heart.

* * * *

As soon as the shallop was ready, Master Jones and Standish resolved to explore more of Cape Cod's coastline. Although the land surrounding Provincetown Harbor was pleasant enough, they hoped they would find somewhere easier and more suitable to build their homes, a place with clearer fields and fewer woods.

With the shallop rebuilt, Jones, Standish, and a party of men set sail from the harbor in mid-December. By then, the *Mayflower* had been at anchor for weeks already; the Pilgrims had at least found fresh water, but they were heading toward the dark heart of winter, and they needed to start building homes if they wanted to survive. Jones knew that there was no chance of returning home himself until spring brought fairer weather. The voyage had already been more than he had bargained for, and it was going to take more still.

The shallop cautiously made its way through the treacherous, wintry waters of Cape Cod, heading southwest in search of a safer harbor. Sailing around the edge of the large Cape Cod Bay, the group soon found another, smaller bay: Wellfleet Bay. It was here that they had their first sighting of the Nauset. As the men sailed toward the bay, they saw a group of people on the beach.

The sighting must have been startling in many ways. Most of the men aboard the shallop had never seen Native Americans before except in drawings, and no one present had seen anyone other than a fellow *Mayflower* passenger in months. The people on the beach were crowded around a beached pilot whale, butchering the animal for its meat, fat, bones, and skin. When the shallop drew nearer, however, the Nauset scattered, leaving the bountiful whale on the beach.

Whales were a significant part of the Nausets' diet, as Jones and the others soon discovered when they dropped anchor in Wellfleet Bay and went out onto the beach. A brief exploration revealed more whale carcasses lying nearby. They were near to a Nauset settlement, that much was certain, and this time, Jones, Standish, and the others hoped to make contact and start trading with them. They knew that cooperation with the Native Americans would be integral to their survival.

What was more, Wellfleet Bay was beautiful. The area surrounding it was more level and welcoming than the hilly surrounds of Provincetown Harbor, and the Nausets had cleared many cornfields in the area, making it even more appealing. Standish was confident that he had found the perfect place for the Pilgrims to start their colony.

Still, even though Standish hoped that they could have peaceful relations with the Nausets, he was deeply cautious. The Pilgrims had been told scary stories about Native Americans, born from the regular conflict between the people of Jamestown and the Powhatan. Bradford, in his journal, noted how they had been warned that Native Americans would capture people and then cut off their limbs and cook and eat them in sight of their still-living victims. There is no evidence to suggest that most Native American tribes were cannibalistic; these stories were hyperbole for the most part, told to make the Native Americans seem less human.

Thus, even though Standish hoped that they could make peace with the Nauset, he also intensely feared them. He'd been told terrifying stories of scalping, cannibalism, and thoughtless killings and not the truth of desperate people defending their homes. So, when Standish and the others settled in to spend the night on the beach, they built a barricade around their camp. The men all had matchlock muskets with them, which were inefficient, especially in the hands of these ordinary people, but potentially deadly. Standish himself carried a flintlock musket, which was never far from his reach.

It turned out that he would have need of it. The group had settled in on the beach when a blood-curdling cry filled the air. "Indians!" shrieked a watchman. "Indians!"

Chaos instantly broke loose. Standish's party, clearly not warriors themselves, had left their armor and weapons lying nearer to the water. They panicked and scattered, rushing for their weapons. At once, a volley of arrows rose from the nearby woods, their hiss in the air a harbinger of danger. They punched into the sand, their deadly tips buried in the dirt, and Standish desperately aimed into the woods and fired. Gunsmoke filled the air, and the crack of the firearm echoed across the beach, shattering the peace of Wellfleet Bay.

The skirmish was a brief one. Almost before the other Pilgrims had managed to get their hands on their weapons, there was a cry of pain from one of the Nauset, likely wounded by Standish. The group of Nauset faded into the trees and melted into the landscape, disappearing from view.

Heart hammering, Standish took quick stock of his men. There were arrows all over the camp, but none of the Pilgrims had been hit. Apart from the wounded Nauset, there were no casualties of what would become known as the "First Encounter."

Nonetheless, Standish knew that things could have gotten ugly. The Nauset in the area had clearly had contact with Europeans before, likely with fishermen who had come to the area for its cod or, even worse, with some Europeans who had made a business of kidnapping Native Americans and selling them as slaves in the Old World. The Nausets knew that Europeans brought only danger with them: disease, murder, kidnapping, and theft. They wanted nothing to do with these Pilgrims, no matter how hungry and desperate they looked. And while this skirmish had ended well for the Pilgrims, it appeared that the Nausets' attack might have been little more than a warning.

It was a warning that Standish took seriously as he looked down at the arrows still jammed into the sand. His men weren't warriors; that much was abundantly clear. They could have all been killed, and the Nauset clearly weren't interested in trade. Beautiful as Wellfleet Bay was, the passengers of the *Mayflower* weren't welcome there, and they would have to move on.

Once again, the shallop set sail, following the curving bay of Cape Cod toward the mainland of North America. Buffeted by winter winds, the tiny boat struggled on through the harsh waters, and everywhere Standish looked, he saw unfamiliar territory. They traveled for two cold, hungry days, sleeping on the shallop under the stars.

Standish was starting to despair of ever finding a new home for his people when, on December 10th, they came upon the most beautiful bay that he had ever seen.

The moment the shallop sailed into the bay, Standish knew that it could be home. Unlike the rest of the densely wooded coastline, there were clear fields here, dusted with frost but ready and waiting for the spring. The curves of the bay welcomed the shallop like open arms, and when Standish and the others landed and started to explore, they found more and more good things—and more and more hope. Fresh water was plentiful; there were springs and streams everywhere. The fields had obviously been cleared by human hands, but there was no sign of human habitation.

Standish had found a home for his people at last, a place where they could build something new, something free. They returned to the shallop and set sail back toward Provincetown Harbor to tell everyone aboard the *Mayflower* the good news.

What Standish didn't know was that the area wasn't uninhabited. Its people were just too weak to fight back.

* * * *

Massasoit, Sachem of the Wampanoags, knew better than most that the Europeans were nothing but trouble.

The Wampanoag had many sachems—local rulers or chiefs—but Massasoit was the leader over them all, a high king of an area spanning much of modern-day Massachusetts. His people had been vast and powerful only a few decades ago when Massasoit was a boy in the 1580s in his birthplace of Montaup (modern-day Bristol, Rhode Island). The Wampanoag was not a single tribe but rather a confederacy of Algonquian-speaking people, and it included tribes such as the Mashpee and Pokanoket. Massasoit himself was a Pokanoket, and he rose to power with the cooperation of the lesser sachems.

With Massasoit at the helm, the Wampanoag prospered. Numbering close to seventy thousand people, they had made a tenuous peace with their more warlike neighbors, the Narragansett. The Wampanoag were a peaceful people, building permanent villages and establishing beautiful farmlands. Like the Nauset, they moved from time to time, living in temporary shelters known as birchbark houses in the summer but constructing winter villages with communal longhouses. While they hunted and fished for their food, they were also farmers and grew beans, sweet potatoes, and the all-important corn, among other things. They used dugout canoes for fishing and wore warm, sturdy clothing made with fur and leather.

The land was bountiful, and the Wampanoag thrived. While there were no colonists in Massasoit's area, there were cod fishermen in the bays, and several of the local sachems began to trade with them. While there were some kidnappings, in general, there was peace between Massasoit and the handful of Europeans that came to his lands.

Yet, what no one knew was that the Europeans had unknowingly brought with them a weapon far deadlier than any gun or blade. They had brought Old World diseases—sicknesses against which the

Wampanoag had absolutely no immunity. Illnesses such as tuberculosis and smallpox had killed millions of people in the Old World, but the robust sailors who had survived to cross the ocean were thoroughly immune to them. Still, they carried those deadly diseases to the New World with them, and they spread through the susceptible native population like wildfire.

In just a few years, Massasoit had seen his people relentlessly decimated. The illness killed without thought, without purpose. Entire villages were destroyed, vibrant communities turned into graveyards of rotting corpses with no one left alive to bury their dead. Children became orphans, wives were widowed, and chaos reigned.

Massasoit could have tried to fight off an invasion. However, this plague was something that no one could stand against. It spared the sachem himself, but it tore his domain to shreds and crushed his people in an iron fist.

When it was all over and the dying finally stopped somewhat, the Wampanoag were a thin shadow of the thriving people that they once had been. Where there had been bustling villages and well-tended farmlands, there were now ghost towns and empty fields. Where there had been laughing children, there were grieving parents. And where there had been a strong and prosperous people, there was a shattered remnant, grieving, sickly, and afraid. Over forty-five thousand people were dead–two-thirds of the population.

Massasoit had survived the epidemic, but now, the Wampanoags' troubles were far from over. Their neighbors, the Narragansett, had fared better during the plague, and they sought to take advantage of the Wampanoags' weakness and attack them to expand their territories. The threat of invasion loomed over the Wampanoags' heads, and Massasoit knew that his people in their weakened state would never be able to fight it off.

Things only got worse when one of the sachems near the coastline, an Abenaki named Samoset, reported the bad news. More Europeans had come to the nearby bay, in an area surrounding one of the villages that had been abandoned after its people were killed by diseases. They had disappeared after a short while, but now they were returning—and this time, they had brought an enormous ship with them. There were women with them, children even.

The news was grim for Massasoit. If these Europeans had brought their families with them, then they weren't just hunters or fishermen passing by to trade and then go back to the Old World. They were colonists.

Massasoit now faced invasion on two different fronts.

* * * *

The *Mayflower* sailed into the pleasant bay on December 18th, 1620, nearly five months after the Pilgrims first departed from Delfshaven. They had been living in the cramped quarters of the gun decks for 149 days, but now, at last, they had reached the place that would become their new home.

As they began to further explore the area, they saw neither hide nor hair of the native people who had cleared these fields. There was an abandoned village nearby; the Pilgrims appear not to have disturbed it, but they must have wondered where all the people had gone. Perhaps they guessed at the gruesome truth: that Old World diseases had rendered two-thirds of the Wampanoag settlements as empty as this one.

In any case, the Pilgrims didn't see any Wampanoag that winter, and they were grateful that there were no attacks such as there had been from the Nauset. Between the lack of resistance from the indigenous people and the clear farmlands, the Pilgrims knew they had finally found a place to call home.

Like many other colonists, they wanted to name their new home after their old one. They would never have left the English shores they treasured if James's anti-Separatist campaign hadn't forced them to go. Ultimately, they decided to name their new bay after the last English shoreline they had seen: Plymouth. And so, Plymouth Colony was born—and it was born into struggle and strife.

The European diseases that had wiped out Massasoit's people did not spare the Pilgrims either. Malnutrition and the cold New England winter—a cold for which the Pilgrims were woefully unprepared—cooked up a deadly concoction of disease aboard the *Mayflower*, which was exacerbated by the cramped and unhygienic conditions. As the Pilgrims began to cut timber and put together the first wattle-and-daub cottages, disease swept through them, and it would devastate them nearly as bad as it had devastated the Wampanoag.

Standish's men were among the first to be affected. On several occasions, as they spent the night on the shore during their expeditions, the temperatures had grown so cold that their wet socks had frozen on their feet. Frostbite was inevitable, and the cold was so terrible that some of the men fainted due to it. They were weak enough as it was. A terrible cough and a raging fever followed close on the heels of that cold.

With every cough, those men were expelling droplets of infection into the air. It spread to the rest of the *Mayflower*'s passengers. Before long, the entire ship was echoing with the sounds of illness, and the Pilgrims had to face the fact that they had lost their race against the cold weather. They would be struggling to build their homes in the very depths of a New England winter.

The extent of that struggle for survival is difficult to comprehend. The cold, the starvation, the unrelenting sickness—it must have been too miserable and frightening and depressing to describe. The colonists had left Delfshaven with so much hope. They had just been looking for somewhere to live out their faith in freedom and peace. Instead, they were struggling to cut wet timber, to dig foundations in frozen ground. The men worked as hard as they could when they were well enough to stand, but they struggled on with burning fevers, with chests ablaze with disease because they had no choice. And when they were no longer able to walk, they tossed and turned in the same uncomfortable bunks that had been their unhappy lot since the summer.

It wasn't long before people started to die. People who had made it through that terrifying voyage were now succumbing quickly to the dreaded disease that stole their breath and ravaged their emaciated bodies. Children were dying as their mothers lay suffering beside them. Men watched their wives melt away before their eyes. Women who had loyally followed their husbands across the stormy ocean were now watching as their last hope of security, their last symbol of normality, faded away.

Bradford's description of that dark time is tragic and sobering. Once people started dying, they died at a terrifying rate. As many as two or three people were dying every day. Burying them was nearly impossible in the frozen ground, and it took up time and energy that was so desperately needed in order to build warm homes to save the ones who were left.

The suffering of the sick was appalling. According to Bradford's account, it was bad enough that many Strangers refused to go near their sick fellows, abandoning them to care for themselves. For the Saints, however, it was time to set their differences aside and tend to whoever needed it, whether they were a Separatist or not. Many Strangers who had joined the *Mayflower* expedition in a bid to give themselves and their families back in England better lives now lost the only lives they had, suffering and alone among people they hardly knew.

There were times when so many of the *Mayflower*'s passengers were sick that only six or seven people were left to tend to the ill. Construction of the settlement ground to a halt for days at a time as the handful of healthy people struggled to care for the dying. The sick were so incapacitated that they couldn't bathe or feed themselves. These patient few, themselves still malnourished and cold even if they weren't sick, were forced to feed the sick, turn them over, strip them of their soiled clothes, clean their filthy bodies, and try to keep them warm.

For the Separatists, too, the losses were absolutely devastating. This congregation had survived so much together. They had attended secret meetings in Brewster's home back in Scrooby. They had smuggled one another across the British Channel to Leiden, risking fines and imprisonment all the way. In Leiden, they had stuck together despite the poverty and alienation that they found there. And they had even survived the trials of the *Speedwell* and the harshness of the open sea. But now they were losing friends and family members. For the Separatists, their congregation had been the one constant through all the trials since King James I first started his campaign against them. And now they were losing the people they loved at an incomprehensible rate.

For Susanna White, the mother of little Peregrine, it meant the loss of her husband. She herself survived and found herself alone to raise her baby boy on a foreign continent. And for Governor John Carver, though he and Catherine both survived, it meant the loss of little Jasper More, the child they'd adopted. Carver had already buried two children back in the Old World; now, in the frigid ground of Plymouth, he laid Jasper to rest too. Young Jasper's two sisters, Ellen and Mary, also perished. They had been the last family that Richard More had left. The boy's parents didn't want him, and now, his siblings were all dead.

Myles Standish and William Bradford also suffered incomprehensible losses. Both had brought wives to the New World, and both lost their wives that dark winter. Dorothy Bradford had drowned back in Provincetown Harbor, her body disappearing into the depths of the sea without a trace. And Rose Standish, who had stood so staunchly by her husband for so long, died aboard the *Mayflower* in late January.

Despite the appalling deaths that continued all around them, the able-bodied colonists continued to work away at building their settlement, desperate to have somewhere to live away from the death ship that the *Mayflower* was fast becoming. Slowly, the settlement began to take shape between two hills. Cole's Hill would become the location for most of the buildings of Plymouth Colony. They were primarily wattle-and-daub cottages, but as time went on, timber buildings began to take shape.

On the other side, Fort Hill, a wooden platform was built overlooking the tiny colony. Here, five cannons were taken from the *Mayflower* and stationed on top of the hill. Peaceful though the Pilgrims hoped their relations with the natives would be, Standish wasn't taking any chances, especially after the "First Encounter."

By the end of February, the buildings were still woefully inadequate. The colonists had planned to finish at least nineteen buildings by that time. Instead, only eleven small buildings clustered miserably around Cole's Hill, with a growing collection of graves lying beside them. Yet, those eleven buildings were almost enough to house the remaining Pilgrims, for of the 102 passengers that had boarded the *Mayflower* in England, only 45 survived that terrible winter.

March brought the first thaw, longer days, and a breath of hope. The disease stopped at last, its deadly work done. The grieving people were able to look forward to their first summer in the New World. But even now—even after financing the voyage, surviving it, and living through that awful winter—trouble still loomed on the horizon. The Wampanoag had noticed the cannons on Fort Hill. And they were desperate to protect themselves against this European threat.

Chapter 7 – The First Thanksgiving

Illustration V: An artist's impression of Tisquantum, who was nicknamed "Squanto" by William Bradford, presumably because his real name was difficult for Englishmen to pronounce.

Massasoit was worried, and he had reason to be.

Spring was coming to Massasoit's domain. The plague had finally stopped attacking his people, but now that the thaw had come, he knew that the Narragansett would soon be planning their next move. And now that the Europeans had built a settlement on the shore, Massasoit's people were caught between two enemies.

None of the Wampanoag had actually spoken to the Europeans yet, but Massasoit had heard the stories. He knew how people had been stolen away by the Europeans and were sold as slaves, of how these barbaric invaders had raped women, desecrated holy sites, and taken land. In fact, one of Massasoit's own subjects, Tisquantum, had been kidnapped by Thomas Hunt and sold as a slave in Spain; he had only recently been able to return to America.

The Europeans' disrespect and their unrelenting savagery had shocked Native American leaders all over the continent. And now, with his people weakened and the Narragansett at their backs, Massasoit knew that they were facing that same terrible threat themselves.

Every report that reached his ears from Wampanoag who had ventured nearer to the European settlement worried him more and more. His fears were confirmed: the Europeans had built a permanent home, and, worse, they had erected a platform with cannons on top of the hill. Massasoit had heard of what cannons could do to a troop of men, how it could rip them to pieces and tear great holes in the earth. Those ugly black cannons on the hilltop were, to Massasoit, a statement of war. These colonists were going to ravage his people just like their diseases; the struggling remnants of the Wampanoag would be butchered and kidnapped, sold and destroyed.

Before March, the Wampanoag had still not yet made real contact with the settlers. They had observed them from afar, always bolting in fear whenever the Europeans came too close; one bold party had stolen some tools left at a worksite and brought them back to their people. As the March days lengthened, however, Massasoit knew that it was time to act.

Even with their small numbers, the Wampanoag could have attacked the colony. They had suffered, thanks to the disease, but there were still several thousand of them; they could have beaten the Pilgrims in battle, even if that meant angering the English Crown itself. But two Native Americans changed Massasoit's mind, two men who would become instrumental in saving the colony: Samoset and Tisquantum.

Samoset was the first Native American to make contact with the Pilgrims. He himself was not native to the Pokanoket region where Massasoit lived. Although Samoset was a minor Abenaki sachem, he was nonetheless part of the Wampanoag confederacy, and he had come to Montaup on a diplomatic visit to Massasoit. Unlike Massasoit, however, he had had direct contact with the English. His domain included the Gulf of Maine, where English fishermen often came to fish the rich and abundant waters. These fishermen had little interest in what happened inland if they were allowed to fish in peace, and so, they had no hostility toward the Abenaki.

Samoset, a fearless young ruler, had spoken with the English on enough occasions that he could speak some of the language. He had also traded with them and enjoyed a friendly drink over a campfire with the fishermen. He suspected that the colonists in the area where the Patuxet lived were more like the fishermen than like the bloodthirsty men of Jamestown. He had a feeling that the Pilgrims were just ordinary people trying to survive. He encouraged Massasoit to talk to the colonists and try to establish peace with them.

The other native was Tisquantum. Tisquantum was either a captive or a refugee among the Wampanoag, and he himself was Patuxet—the last living Patuxet, in fact. The very village that the Pilgrims had discovered was the place where he had grown up; it had once been a thriving community of around two thousand people. Tisquantum's fate took a sad turn when he was only a young man.

If anyone had reason to hate the Europeans in general, and the English in particular, it was Tisquantum. Born around 1580, he had been a young man in his twenties when he was kidnapped in 1605 by Captain George Weymouth. Weymouth was exploring the northern New England area, where Tisquantum and some others happened to be on a hunting expedition. He wanted to kidnap some "Indians" in order to show them to the owner of the company that had sent him to the New World: Sir Ferdinando Gorges. To Weymouth and Gorges, these native people were nothing more than a fascinating novelty.

Tisquantum was among the unlucky number that was forced into a ship and carried across the Atlantic, an experience that had been terrifying enough for the Pilgrims, who had boarded the *Mayflower* voluntarily. Tisquantum was thrown around in a dark hold, treated as something inferior, and never told what was happening to him.

Traumatized and malnourished, Tisquantum arrived in England later that year, only to be given to Gorges as though he was nothing more than a trinket from the New World. Gorges made it his mission to turn this fascinating novelty into a "civilized" member of society, and Tisquantum learned to speak fluent English when he was held captive by Gorges.

Nine years after being dragged to the Old World, Tisquantum finally had an opportunity to return home. John Smith recognized Tisquantum's value as a guide and interpreter in the New World, so he took him back across the Atlantic—this time as a free man—in order to help out near Jamestown in 1614. Sadly, for Tisquantum, he had only a bare taste of freedom and no contact with his home tribe. Thomas Hunt, another explorer, had determined to add to his cargo of fish by taking some Native Americans back to the Old World to sell as slaves. He deceived some members of a local tribe by inviting them aboard his ship to trade furs; Tisquantum likely came aboard as an interpreter. But no trade took place. Instead, Hunt closed up his ship and sailed to Spain, taking the Native Americans with him—including Tisquantum—to sell at a handsome profit.

Hunt was hoping to feather his nest at the expense of these innocent people, and he sold several of them at the Strait of Gibraltar on his return to Europe. A group of Spanish monks, however, were determined to foil his nefarious plans. When they saw the terrified and confused Native Americans being sold off helplessly to uncertain fates, they refused to stand by and watch.

The monks intervened, putting a stop to Hunt's schemes by bringing Tisquantum and a handful of others back to the monastery with them. These monks were powerless to send Tisquantum home, but they did continue his English education, and they also gave him the freedom to do as he pleased.

Only five years later, in 1619, Tisquantum managed to get himself hired again as a guide and interpreter, traveling back to the New World with an enterprising adventurer. This time, he made it back to Cape Cod at last.

Fourteen years after he had been abducted, Tisquantum finally walked back into the village of Patuxet, the homeland he had been longing for ever since that dreadful day. But if he had been dreaming of being welcomed home by friends and family, his dreams were horrendously dashed.

It is difficult to imagine just how tragic that moment must have been for Tisquantum. He had suffered so much and endured such hardship in order to come back home. And now, even though the fields were as green as he remembered, the water as perfectly smooth, and the woods as coolly shaded, Patuxet had changed. The very heart of the land had been torn out, its soul ripped away.

Everyone was dead.

Tisquantum walked into an abandoned village. There were no people. No animals. No crops. Only some bones—the remnants of a plague so vicious that no one had been left to bury the dead. Smallpox had destroyed the entire village, Tisquantum's whole family, his tribe, his people, even his identity. The moment was meant to be one of a joyous homecoming, but instead, it was the day that Tisquantum learned that he was the very last Patuxet.

And so Tisquantum found himself in Massasoit's court. The Europeans had essentially ruined his life in every sense of the word: they had kidnapped him twice, enslaved him, passed him about like a mere object, and then brought disease to the New World that had wiped out his entire family. Yet, for whatever reason, Tisquantum pleaded on behalf of the colonists. He asked Massasoit to give him the grace of meeting with them first to attempt to establish a peace.

It was not only for compassionate reasons that Massasoit agreed with Samoset and Tisquantum. He knew that he could not afford to be fighting a war on two fronts. What was more, if he could make peace with the Europeans, perhaps they could be persuaded to help him if the Narragansetts attacked.

Massasoit agreed to try to make a treaty with the Europeans, and he sent Samoset to speak with them.

The young sachem was all too happy to be entrusted with this task. He was absolutely fearless, and he harbored less resentment of the Europeans than Tisquantum did, so he set out for Patuxet with a swagger in his step.

* * * *

Spring had brought hope to Plymouth Colony but also fear.

The surviving colonists, about fifty in all, were half-amazed, half-relieved that they had made it through that unbearable winter. Their sick were recovering, with most of them finally able to get to work again, and they had started to till the empty fields surrounding the mysteriously abandoned village. Governor John Carver, albeit not in good health, had succeeded in keeping order between the Saints and Strangers.

The great threat that faced them now was the Native Americans.

Myles Standish, grieving though he was, knew that the cannons alone would not be enough to ward off a full attack by some outraged tribe. He would have to convert this batch of ordinary people into warriors.

Accordingly, Standish selected a handful of men and started training them in the art of war. They were a motley bunch, but he was determined to make it work.

The colonists were, in fact, in the very middle of their training when a tall, young Native American man came swaggering right into Plymouth Colony. He came so boldly that they might have fired the cannons on him if it wasn't for the fact that his hands were empty (although he had a bow and two arrows in his quiver) and that he was alone. As it was, the women and children ran, panicking for their homes, while the male colonists gathered warily around him, nervous but hoping that their plan of making peace with the natives would finally be given a chance to succeed.

To their shock, the Native American greeted them in broken English and introduced himself as Samoset, a lord of a nearby area—and then asked them if they had any beer. The request put them instantly at ease. The colonists were running short on beer, but they offered him water, butter and cheese from the cow that had survived the journey, some biscuits, and some duck. When the wind rose, they also offered him a coat—a well-meaning, if perhaps unnecessary gesture. Samoset cheerfully accepted these and started to tell them all about the new land they had come to.

Something that had been concerning the colonists was the abandoned village. They wanted to know who this land belonged to. Samoset put their minds at ease, telling them about the plague and the death of the Patuxet. In the colonists' eyes, that made this land their own.

They visited with Samoset all afternoon and into the evening. Although the colonists remained wary, Samoset's cheerful, free manner started to put them at ease. He spent the night in Stephen Hopkin's home—albeit under some guard.

Samoset had told Governor Carver that Massasoit wanted to make peace with them. This was a massive relief, and Carver sent him back to the sachem with a few small gifts.

A few days later, Samoset returned, bringing with him a few other men and also the tools that had been taken from Plymouth Colony. This gesture of goodwill served to put the colonists even more at ease. Samoset also brought some furs in the hope of trading with the colonists. Carver was delighted by this. Another threat that had been looming over Plymouth Colony was their mounting debt to the Merchant Adventurers, and the trade in furs would be their only real hope of paying the company back. However, it happened to be a Sunday, and Carver couldn't accept the furs on a day he considered to be holy. Instead, he offered the men something to eat and encouraged them to come back later.

When Massasoit and his delegation arrived on March 22nd, 1621, Carver and the others were ready and relieved to be friends with their new neighbors. Massasoit's impressive group, which arrived with considerable pomp, dwarfed the pitiful scrapings of the trumpet and drum that announced the arrival of the sickly Governor Carver. Still, Massasoit saw potential in the colonists and the potential for an alliance that could ensure their mutual survival. After sharing a meal together and exchanging some gifts, Carver and Massasoit signed a peace treaty that would last for fifty years.

The peace itself was a gift that contributed to Plymouth Colony's survival. But Massasoit also left behind another gift, one that would finally ensure that the colonists could make a home for themselves in the New World: Tisquantum.

It's unknown whether Tisquantum willingly went to live with the colonists or whether Massasoit made him do it. Perhaps he joined them hoping to be free of Massasoit, or perhaps his motivation was a deeper one. Tisquantum had walked the hills of Patuxet, his homeland, and heard only silence after the terrible plague. He had known unutterable grief and loneliness. He had been robbed of his entire family, his whole people.

But now, there were people in Patuxet again. There were children, dogs, women, livestock, and fishermen. They were far from perfect. They weren't Patuxet. They weren't even Native American. But for Tisquantum, they had the potential to be a family for him, despite their white skins. And so, after the celebrations had died down and Massasoit and Samoset had returned to their domains, Tisquantum threw himself wholeheartedly into the task of helping the Pilgrims survive.

Bradford would later call Tisquantum "an instrument of God." His presence in the colony was nothing short of miraculous. The Pilgrims had been trying to grow the corn they'd stolen from the Nauset, but it wouldn't come up, no matter what they did. It was Tisquantum who showed them how to plant and fertilize it with the abundant fish they could catch in Plymouth Harbor. He showed them how to trap and skin beaver for their lucrative fur. He showed them how to grow all the vegetables that his tribe had always grown, and so, thanks to one man's compassion, Plymouth Colony began to thrive at last.

* * * *

Almost a year had passed since the Pilgrims came to Plymouth, and the air was thick with festivity.

Fall had come to New England, all green and gold and breathtaking scarlet. The gathering of houses that formed Plymouth Colony had grown; the cannons on Fort Hill were dusty with disuse. The storehouses were full to the brim. The fields were empty, their abundant crops gathered safely for the winter. Livestock grazed on the hillsides, thriving and well. And in the middle of the colony, a great feast was underway.

Everyone was there—everyone who had survived, anyway. There was William Brewster, who had now become the pastor of Plymouth Colony, with Mary and little Richard More by his side; the widowed Susanna White, one of only four married women who had survived the winter and who had been faced with the challenge of cooking a vast feast with only a handful of people to help her; John Howland, now an important figure in the colony and one who had been instrumental in negotiating peace with the Wampanoag; Myles Standish, stalwart as ever; Tisquantum, the hero of Plymouth Colony; Massasoit, with a huge delegation of Native Americans, which outnumbered the colonists almost two to one; and William Bradford.

Sadly, John and Catherine Carver had died in the spring of 1621. It was as though Carver had held on for just long enough to see peace between the colonists and the Native Americans. He was not there to see this great harvest celebration, but William Bradford had become the governor of Plymouth Colony in his stead, and he would lead the colony for nearly thirty years to come.

It was with a full heart that William Bradford looked out over the great feast that Susanna White and the other women had prepared. There were vegetables and grains from the colonists' fields, fish and shellfish from the bay, fruits and nuts from their orchards, and venison from their new friends, the Wampanoag. Everywhere Bradford looked, he saw smiling faces. Laughing children. Happy couples. Cheerful men.

He was a long, long way from Nottinghamshire now, and his faith had taken him a long way from home. But now, at last, the Separatists had a home of their own.

That was enough reason to be thankful. And so, hundreds of years later, a harvest festival a little like this one would become an annual American tradition: Thanksgiving.

Conclusion

The name *Mayflower* would become one of the most famous in history. In fact, it is debatable whether any other ship is as well known across the world. She was a very ordinary ship, an underdog, honestly, compared with the other vessels that had to make their way across the Atlantic. Yet her voyage was a historic one.

Perhaps it was the *Mayflower*'s mediocrity that made her voyage so extraordinary. The Pilgrims, too, were just ordinary people. They weren't adventurers, sailors, or wealthy merchants. They were just farmers and fishermen with families to feed, people who wanted nothing more than to practice their faith in peace and who were willing to do whatever it took to make that happen.

As for the *Mayflower* herself, she would only become famous many years later, after Plymouth Colony had endured for decades and the Pilgrims had all died and been buried on Cole's Hill, along with the victims of that deadly plague in the winter of 1620. Her end was tragically ignominious.

In April 1621, once most of Master Jones's crew had recovered from their illness, he was finally able to set sail toward home. This time, the journey was an easy one. Only a few weeks later, on May 5th, 1621, the weary *Mayflower* finally sailed back into her home port of

Rotherhithe. But neither Jones nor his ship was the same as they had been when they had left England. The journeys had taken a terrible toll on them both. The *Mayflower* was all but falling apart, her timbers creaky, her mainmast cracked, and her crew racked by disease.

Josian Jones hardly recognized her own husband when he returned to her arms at last. The once-sprightly captain was a mere sickly shadow of the man he had once been, and his health would continue to fail. He was home for only ten months before the sickness finally won out. He died in March 1622, leaving the *Mayflower* to his grieving widow.

At first, Josian wanted little to do with the ship. Her other owners, too, appear to have more or less forgotten about her. She lay neglected in port until Josian finally had her appraised in 1624, hoping to settle her husband's estate. Sadly, there was nothing more to be done with the *Mayflower*. She would never sail again, and although her ultimate fate is not known, she was likely broken up and sold as scrap lumber.

It was a tragic ending for a ship that had carried the founders of a nation across the Atlantic. But although the *Mayflower*'s timbers have likely long since rotted into nothing, her story lives on. It has endured for generations, and it will endure for many, many more.

Here's another book by Captivating History that you might like

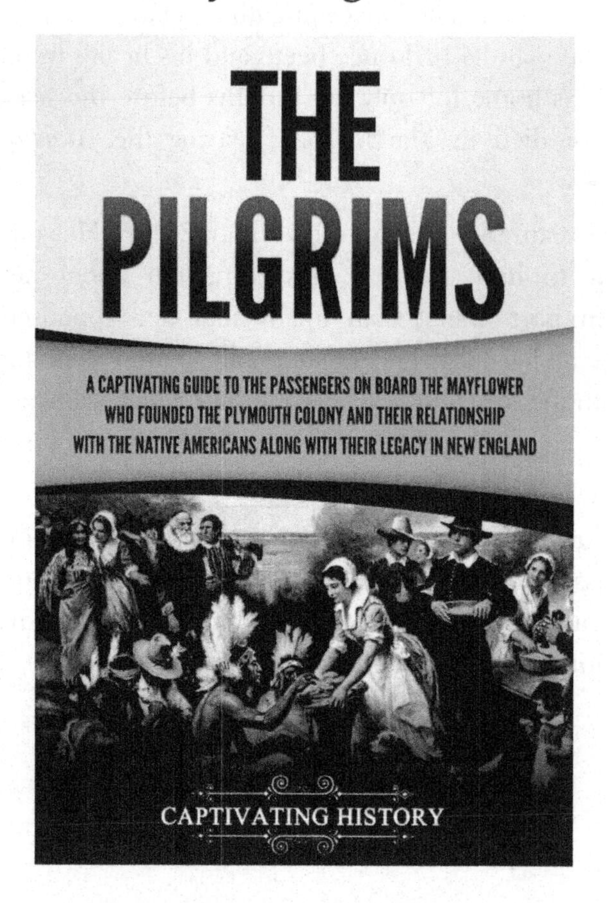

Free Bonus from Captivating History (Available for a Limited time)

Hi History Lovers!

Now you have a chance to join our exclusive history list so you can get your first history ebook for free as well as discounts and a potential to get more history books for free! Simply visit the link below to join.

Captivatinghistory.com/ebook

Also, make sure to follow us on Facebook, Twitter and Youtube by searching for Captivating History.

Sources

Anonymous 2017, *New World Economics: How the Pilgrims Financed Their Journey*, New Era Debt Solutions, viewed May 2021, <https://neweradebtsolutions.com/new-world-economics-pilgrims-financed-journey/>

Anonymous 2011, *Church of England*, British Broadcasting Commission, viewed May 2021, <https://www.bbc.co.uk/religion/religions/christianity/cofe/cofe_1.shtml>

History.com Editors 2020, *Martin Luther Posts His 95 Theses*, A&E Television Networks, viewed May 2021, <https://www.history.com/this-day-in-history/martin-luther-posts-95-theses>

Petruzzello, M. 2016, *Separatist*, Encyclopedia Britannica, viewed May 2021, <https://www.britannica.com/topic/Separatists>

Voiland, A. 2016, *Holland: First Stop for the Pilgrims*, NASA Earth Observatory, viewed May 2021, <https://earthobservatory.nasa.gov/images/91317/holland-first-stop-for-the-pilgrims>

Pruitt, S. 2020, *Colonists at the First Thanksgiving Were Mostly Men Because Women Had Perished*, A&E Television Networks, viewed

June 2021, <https://www.history.com/news/first-thanksgiving-colonists-native-americans-men>

Biography.com Editors 2020, *Squanto*, A&E Television Networks, viewed June 2021, <https://www.biography.com/political-figure/squanto>

Siteseen Limited 2012, *Wampanoag Tribe*, Siteseen Limited, viewed June 2021, <https://www.warpaths2peacepipes.com/indian-tribes/wampanoag-tribe.htm>

History.com Editors 2020, *Mayflower Docks at Plymouth Harbor*, A&E Television Networks, viewed June 2021, <https://www.history.com/this-day-in-history/mayflower-docks-at-plymouth-harbor>

Brosnahan, T., *Massasoit, Wampanoag Sachem*, New England Travel Planner, viewed June 2021, <https://newenglandtravelplanner.com/people/massasoit.html>

Gillo-Whitaker, D. 2020, *Biography of Chief Massasoit, Native American Hero*, ThoughtCo, viewed June 2021, <https://www.thoughtco.com/profile-chief-massasoit-2477989>

Britannica, The Editors of Encyclopedia 2013, *Nauset*, Encyclopedia Britannica, viewed June 2021, <https://www.britannica.com/topic/Nauset>

Seay, B. 2019, *Reframing the Story of the First Encounter Between the Native Americans and the Pilgrims*, GBH News, viewed June 2021, <https://www.wgbh.org/news/local-news/2019/11/28/reframing-the-story-of-the-first-encounter-between-native-americans-and-the-pilgrims>

Harrigan, S. 2012, *First Encounter*, HistoryNet, viewed June 2021, <https://www.historynet.com/first-encounter.htm>

History.com Editors 2019, *Plymouth Colony*, A&E Television Networks, viewed June 2021, <https://www.history.com/topics/colonial-america/plymouth>

Bradford, W. 1656, *Of Plymouth Plantation,* excerpts by National Humanities Center, viewed June 2021, <https://nationalhumanitiescenter.org/pds/amerbegin/settlement/text1/BradfordPlymouthPlantation.pdf>

Beyond the Pilgrim Story 2012, *John & Catherine Carver,* Pilgrim Hall Museum, viewed June 2021, <https://pilgrimhall.org/john_catherine_carver.htm>

History.com Editors 2020, *Mayflower Compact,* A&E Television Networks, viewed June 2021, <https://www.history.com/topics/colonial-america/mayflower-compact>

Roos, D. 2020, *The Pilgrims' Miserable Journey Aboard Mayflower,* A&E Television Networks, viewed June 2021, <https://www.history.com/news/mayflower-journey-pilgrims-america?li_source=LI&li_medium=m2m-rcw-history>

Klein, C. 2019, *Did the Pilgrims intend to land at Plymouth?,* A&E Television Networks, viewed June 2021, <https://www.history.com/news/did-the-pilgrims-intend-to-land-at-plymouth>

Harris, D., *The More Children's Story,* Shropshire Mayflower, viewed June 2021, <http://shropshiremayflower.com/the-four-more-children/>

History.com Editors 2019, *John Smith,* A&E Television Networks, viewed June 2021, <https://www.history.com/topics/colonial-america/john-smith>

Spencer, A. 2019, *New Evidence: Was Thomas Weston, Seventeenth Century London Merchant among the First to Sail Fish to Virginia's Starving Colonists?,* Global Maritime History, viewed June 2021, <http://globalmaritimehistory.com/thomas_weston_merchant/>

Mark, J. J. 2020, *Mayflower Passengers & Crew,* World History, viewed June 2021,

<https://www.worldhistory.org/article/1631/mayflower-passengers--crew/>

Mullane, J. 2017, *The Speedwell, forgotten ship of the Pilgrims' voyage*, Courier Times, viewed June 2021, <https://www.buckscountycouriertimes.com/news/20171122/speedwell-forgotten-ship-of-pilgrims-voyage/1>

Britannica, Editors of Encyclopedia, *John Robinson*, Encyclopedia Britannica, viewed June 2021, <https://www.britannica.com/biography/John-Robinson-English-minister>

Moffitt, D. 2020, *Myles Standish: The Lancashire man who founded modern America*, LancsLive, viewed June 2021, <https://www.lancs.live/news/lancashire-news/myles-standish-lancashire-man-who-18048918>

Worrall, S. 2006, *Pilgrims' Progress*, Smithsonian Magazine, viewed June 2021, <https://www.smithsonianmag.com/history/pilgrims-progress-135067108/>

History.com Editors 2018, *William Bradford*, A&E Television Networks, viewed June 2021, <https://www.history.com/topics/colonial-america/william-bradford>

History.com Editors 2019, *The Pilgrims*, A&E Television Networks, viewed June 2021, <https://www.history.com/topics/colonial-america/pilgrims>

Illustration I: By wikitravel:user:OldPine, CC BY-SA 1.0, https://commons.wikimedia.org/w/index.php?curid=986647

Illustration II: https://commons.wikimedia.org/wiki/File:Embarkation_of_the_Pilgrims.jpg

Illustration III: https://commons.wikimedia.org/wiki/File:After_the_Storm,_by_William_Bradford.JPG

Illustration IV:
https://commons.wikimedia.org/wiki/File:Mayflower_in_Plymouth_Harbor,_by_William_Halsall.jpg

Made in United States
Orlando, FL
12 April 2022